SHORT WALKS FROM

Surrey Pubs

D1078429

Derek Palmer

COUNTRYSIDE BOOKS
NEWBURY, BERKSHIRE

First Published 1995
© Derek Palmer 1995

COUNTRYSIDE BOOKS
3 Catherine Road
Newbury, Berkshire

ISBN 1 85306 363 0

Designed by Mon Mohan
Cover illustration by Colin Doggett
Photographs by the author
Maps by Brenda Palmer

Produced through MRM Associates Ltd., Reading
Typeset by Paragon Typesetters, Clwyd
Printed by Woolnough Bookbinding Ltd., Irthlingborough

Contents

Introduction 6

Walk 1 The Sands: The Barley Mow (1½ miles or
3 miles) 8

2 Haslemere: The White Horse Hotel (3 miles) 12

3 Brook: The Dog and Pheasant (2½ miles or
3 miles) 16

4 Pirbright: The Cricketers (2½ miles) 20

5 Chobham: The Four Horseshoes (3 miles) 25

6 Horsell Common: The Bleak House (3½ miles) 29

7 Sutton Green: The Fox and Hounds (3½ miles) 34

8 Guildford: The Jolly Farmer (4 miles) 39

9 Merrow: The Horse and Groom (3 miles) 44

10 Ripley: The Talbot Hotel (2½ miles) 48

11 Weybridge: The Lincoln Arms (3 miles) 53

12 Wotton: The Wotton Hatch (2½ miles or
4½ miles) 57

13 Ockley: The Old School House (3 miles) 62

14 Newdigate: The Six Bells (4½ miles) 67

15   Brockham: The Dukes Head (3¾ miles)   71

16   Walton on the Hill: The Chequers (3½ miles)   76

17   Charlwood: The Greyhound (3½ miles)   80

18   Godstone: The Bell Inn (2½ miles)   84

19   Chelsham: The Bull Inn (2½ miles)   88

20   Dormansland: The Plough Inn
      (4 miles or 5½ miles)   92

Publisher's Note

We hope that you obtain considerable enjoyment from this book; great care has been taken in its preparation. However, changes of landlord and actual closures are sadly not uncommon. Likewise, although at the time of publication all routes followed public rights of way or permitted paths, diversion orders can be made and permissions withdrawn.

We cannot of course be held responsible for such diversion orders and any resultant inaccuracies in the text which result from these or any other changes to the routes nor any damage which might result from walkers trespassing on private property. We are anxious that all details covering the walks and the pubs are kept up to date and would therefore welcome information from readers which would be relevant to future editions.

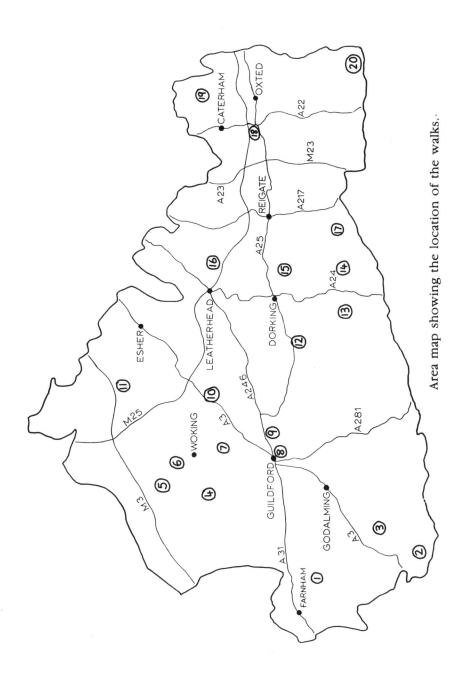

Area map showing the location of the walks.

Introduction

Do you have not much time to spare yet would welcome some fresh air away from the hustle and bustle of everyday life?

Are you looking for something different to entertain the family?

Do you enjoy eating out but need to burn up a few calories to justify it?

Are you looking for an introduction to country walking?

If you can answer 'yes' to any of these questions, you have chosen the right book!

All these short walks are suitable for the less dedicated rambler and will provide an hour or two of pleasant walking in lovely countryside. Surrey has a variety of scenery ranging from the sandy heathlands, with their heather and gorse, in the west to the clayey woodlands and fields of the Weald to the south. Then there is the grass-covered chalk of the North Downs. Important for the beautiful wild flowers, including rare species of orchid, the Downs form a backdrop to many of the walks. The routes are spread throughout the county and enable you to experience much of this diversity.

I have tried to select fairly flat routes with which anyone of average fitness, of any age, should have no difficulty. Fortunately, this has not had to be at the expense of good views, and you will find many to savour. Water is magnetic in its appeal to young and old, so I make no excuse for including the towpaths of the pretty river Wey and Navigation and the river Thames in four of the walks. Other routes pass village ponds or maybe just a gurgling stream.

Apart from the familiar farm animals in the fields you will discover rare breeds of sheep and pigs and even a donkey sanctuary. You could also be lucky enough to spot some infrequently seen wildlife. Points of interest along the way, such as historic manor and farmhouses, ancient churches, watermills and Iron Age forts, are mentioned in the text. Many of the places passed through have interesting connections with well-known characters and these, too, are mentioned. Often there are further attractions such as museums and zoos to visit.

Two Ordnance Survey maps cover most of the county and all but one of the areas used: Landrangers 186 (Aldershot and Guildford) and 187 (Dorking and Reigate). They will help you find the pubs and the starting points of the walks, for which a map reference is given, and will also enable you to follow the routes. If you enjoy map-reading and want to make your walk even more pleasurable as you go along you may wish to buy an OS Pathfinder map, the details of which are given for each walk. At double the scale of the Landranger, these maps show much more detail. Maps are certainly not essential since the detailed instructions for each walk, coupled with the use of the sketch map, will ensure you have no difficulty in finding your way.

The mileage for each walk is given and should be correct to within ¼ mile or so. Allow extra time for dallying at viewpoints, taking photographs, having refreshments and stopping at places of interest.

Even on a relatively short walk, and particularly on warm days, you can soon get thirsty. So it's a good idea to carry a flask or a bottle of water with you. Also remember your waterproof, just in case!

You may not have proper walking shoes or boots and in summer a pair of trainers will probably provide perfectly adequate footwear. However, in winter, and at any time after prolonged rain, paths and particularly bridleways, are going to be muddy. Proper walking boots are undoubtedly best but you could possibly try wellingtons. As long as they fit well they could be fine for the shortest walks and young children will love to put them to good use. By the way, do remember that most pubs are carpeted, so please don't forget to change your footwear before you go in.

The landlords are willing for their car parks to be used whilst you are on the walks, but please seek permission before you set off.

All of the pubs have been chosen not only because they are close to pleasant walking country but also because they offer good value for money in a welcoming and relaxing atmosphere. They each have their individual character and many offer those little extras which make your visit memorable and more enjoyable – log fires to warm your toes in winter, perhaps, cosy armchairs in which to lounge, newspapers to read and games to play.

These days pubs vie with each other to produce good meals at reasonable prices. If the menu is extensive, it cannot be expected that everything is home-prepared and cooked, but in these pubs I found that a high proportion of the dishes were home-made. The variety of food offered is sometimes enormous, but you will always find familiar favourites on the menu – particularly satisfying if you are with young children. Some pubs even have a special menu for children. However, if you are looking for something a bit different, you may well spot what you are after on the specials board. In some cases the chefs have made their reputation with certain dishes and these are always well worth trying.

My thanks to my wife, Brenda, who not only assisted me in obtaining the pub information and checking the routes but also drew the maps. To her I dedicate this book.

Derek Palmer
Spring 1995

The Sands
The Barley Mow

1

The Barley Mow sits prominently in the little village of The Sands, which derives its name from the gravel quarrying that once took place in this area and still does in the sister village of Seale. Although small, the village not only has a pub and a pretty, diminutive church, but also boasts a post office and store.

Barley Mow (Mow is correctly pronounced Mao as in Chairman) refers to a stack of barley, the main ingredient of good beer. In times past farm workers danced around it whilst the farmer stood on top, quaffing from a giant pot of brew yielded by the previous crop, and the gathering of the crop was a time of great revelry. The pub sign, depicting the jolly scene and painted in 1975, is based on an old painting to be found on the pub wall. The pub, whose history goes back over 200 years, is quite small and consequently gets very full, particularly at weekends. Much memorabilia and many illustrations on the walls depict a horse-racing connection, the present landlord having been a jump jockey and trainer during the 1960s and 70s. He once rode in the Grand National.

Most of the food here is home-prepared and cooked and besides the bar menu, which includes the usual pub snacks, there's a specials board with eight to ten main dishes as well as starters and sweets. The beef in beer and lasagne are two dishes that prove particularly popular. This is a Courage house and the regular real ales are Courage Best and John Smith's Bitter and there is always one, and sometimes two, guest ales, such as Wadworth 6X. The draught cider is Scrumpy Jack and the draught stout Beamish. In addition to the bar there is 'the end room', used as an area for eating and where children dining with parents are welcome. Dogs are not barred, but are not encouraged either, unless they are clean, dry and well-behaved. There is a small beer garden at the rear and swings and things are provided for the children's entertainment.

The pub is open on Monday to Saturday from 11.30 am to 2.30 pm and 6 pm to 11 pm, and on Sundays from 12 noon to 3 pm and, in summer, from 7 pm to 10.30 pm. Food is served on Monday to Saturday 12 noon to 2 pm (cold snacks after 2 pm) and 6.30 pm to 9.30 pm, and on Sunday from 12 noon to 2.30 pm and 7 pm to 9 pm. (Note: the pub is not open at all on Sunday evenings outside British Summer Time.)

Telephone: 01252 782200.

How to get there: The Sands is 3 miles east of Farnham and is sign-posted from the A31 Hogs Back (Farnham to Guildford road) and the B3001 (Farnham to Elstead road). Once you have found the village you will easily find the pub.

Parking: The pub's car park is not over large but, with permission, you are welcome to use it whilst on your walk.

Length of the walk: The walk is about 3 miles in total, but it may be reduced to half if you only have time for a short stroll. OS maps: Landranger 186 or Pathfinder 1225 (inn GR 882464).

If you choose a good day, your short climb to the top of Crooksbury Hill will be repaid with some excellent views, maybe as far as the South Downs in Hampshire.

The Walk

1 *For the shorter, 1½-mile, walk from the pub,* turn right along the road for about 250 yards and continue from point 3.

For the longer walk, turn left along the road for about ⅓ mile, going over a crossroads on your way. You reach Blighton Lane and turn right. You are on a stretch of the North Downs Way here and almost immediately pass the clubhouse of Farnham Golf Club, with the first tee right opposite. After about ⅓ mile, where the road curves left, turn right over a stile to join a signposted public footpath. Continue along

the edge of the golf course, passing a magnificent mansion on your left. In about a ⅓ mile you will reach a road.

2 The North Downs Way continues ahead, but you turn right along the road, switching sides as necessary. You will find later that this road cuts through the golf course. When the road turns sharply right you leave it by going straight ahead on a footpath and on through a barrier. Continue along the side of a recreation field and in the corner join a path running under the trees and leading you out to a road.

3 Cross the road to the bridleway opposite, Long Hill, which also gives access to several smart houses. In about ⅓ mile you reach a house on the left, Coedgae. Just beyond it turn right through a gate onto another bridleway, which you will later discover is called Crooksbury Lane. In about another ⅓ mile you will reach a road.

Church of the Good Shepherd, The Sands.

Cross over to the bridleway opposite and soon reach a fork where you bear left, uphill. Where your path starts to descend, leave it by turning right and climb to the top of Crooksbury Hill. 'As high as Crooksbury Hill' is an old Surrey saying.

4   At the summit (some 500 ft) check out the distances on the toposcope, supported by the now redundant triangulation pillar. A very straight-flying crow would travel the miles quoted to arrive at the various well-known places of interest mentioned. Suitably rested, turn right to take the path opposite the best of the views. At an immediate fork keep right on the main path and commence your descent, aided by the occasional wooden step. At the next fork you keep left, still on the main path and, at the bottom of the steep slope, turn left and left again on the bridleway, marked 'P2'. The slope is much more gentle now and you join the bridleway, '341', by turning right. At the next fork keep to your right and come down to a small parking area and a road. Turn right and shortly reach a crossroads where you go straight ahead for just a few yards to see the Church of the Good Shepherd, dated 1875. Retrace your steps to the crossroads and turn left, back to the Barley Mow which is now well in view.

2 Haslemere
The White Horse Hotel

The White Horse Hotel enjoys a prominent position at the bottom of Haslemere's attractive High Street, just across the road from the old town hall, which was built in 1814. There has been a tavern on the site for three centuries or more and it was used as a coaching house. The Palladian façade is in keeping with the generally mid 18th-century, Georgian style of its neighbours. The interior is more akin to a city pub, with turn-of-the-century decor and art deco stained glass much in evidence. The pub is large and roomy with plenty of tables, so you shouldn't have any difficulty in finding somewhere to sit, and there is a 'no smoking' area. On fine days the seating outside adds to the pleasure as you enjoy your food and drink whilst watching the world pass by.

Besides being a 'Big Steak' pub with all that promises, the kitchen offers many home-cooked specialities, including very tasty soups and curries. Veggies are well catered for and, for those who consider it important, the landlady goes to a lot of trouble to produce some calorie-counted meals. Children have their own 'Little Monster' menu with plenty of choices. The cask-conditioned real ale regulars are Friary, Tetley and Burton and monthly-changed guest ales come from all over the UK. Olde English cider comes through a pump and a medium red and a dry white wine are similarly dispensed. Children are permitted in all parts of the pub away from the bar.

The pub is open on Monday to Saturday from 11 am to 11 pm and on Sunday from 12 noon to 3 pm and 7 pm to 10.30 pm. Food, and this includes the full menu all day, is served on Monday to Saturday from 12 noon to 9.30 pm and on Sunday from 12 noon to 2.30 pm and 7 pm to 9 pm.

Telephone: 01428 642103.

How to get there: If travelling south on the A3 from Guildford, leave at the exit for Milford and follow signs to Haslemere on the A286 for approximately 7 miles. You will find the pub on the left almost at the bottom of the High Street.

Parking: You are welcome to use the pub's car park whilst on your walk but you need to let the staff know.

Length of the walk: 3 miles. OS maps: Landranger 186 or Pathfinder 1245 (inn GR 905328).

Within a few minutes of leaving the bustling main street of this attractive country town you are led into tranquil meadows where busy streets and traffic seem miles away. At the far extremity of the route you will be pleasantly surprised to find a peaceful lake where wildfowl abound.

The Walk

1 From the pub turn right up the High Street until you are opposite the Georgian Hotel. (By the side of the latter hotel the Greensand Way, which we encounter on many of our walks, commences its 55-mile route to the county border with Kent.) Turn right down Well Lane, leading to Haslemere's town well. From medieval times until the late 19th-century it was one of the town's few public sources of water. The path also leads to Swan Barn Walk, a short local walking route. Pass a parking area, bear right past two seats and, after passing a third seat, turn left through a wooden barrier. Continue straight across a field towards a waymark on a short post in a dip and on towards another barrier leading to a rough track. Turn left on the track, which for a short stretch is concreted, and arrive at some wooden buildings.

2 Go through a barrier and along some woods to another barrier, where you bear left across a field. Go over a stile and footbridge into Witley Copse and Mariners Rewe, continuing straight ahead. Almost immediately, another path comes in from the left. You leave the woods through a barrier and go along the left perimeter of a field to

13

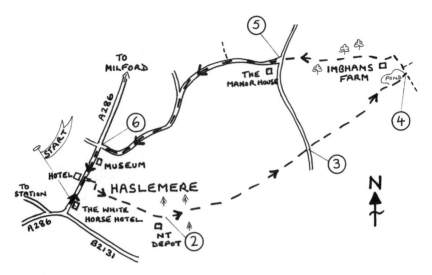

another barrier and pass a seat on your right. Go over a sleeper bridge and up some steps to the next barrier, following a muddy stream down on your left and continuing along the side of the next field. Go through another set of barriers with a sleeper bridge and bear left along the next field to yet another barrier by a farm gate. Continue straight ahead on a well-defined track and, when this reaches some houses, look for a stile on the left. Join a path under trees which later becomes fenced on both sides and leads to a road via a kissing gate.

3 Cross the road to a small gate by a fingerpost and pass The White House on your right. Join a tarred driveway and in a little less than ½ mile reach some farm buildings. Ignore a turning on the left and remain on the farm track as it curves left. Very shortly you come to an attractive lake which was created as a hammer pond, used by the former ironworks at Imbhams. The picturesque buildings on the far side now form the farm taking the same name. You soon reach a T-junction.

4 Turn left on the bridleway, ignoring an immediate right turn. The track soon turns left, passing the farm buildings where you follow the waymarked public bridleway. Pass a woodshed on your right and bear right to continue along the right side of a field, shortly entering woodland. Proceed along an upward sloping path, eventually reaching the top of the slope where you commence your descent. Go through a five-barred gate and down the side of a field. The next gate (or stile) leads you out to a road.

5 Cross to the road opposite, Three Gates Lane, and climb past an attractive property on the left, The Manor House. It is not possible to

14

Imbhams Farm, near Haslemere.

see much of it through the magnificent gates but it is one of only five houses in Surrey exhibiting the fine quality of Carolean architecture. Later you will pass Meadfields, which formed part of the estate of Sir Robert Hunter, co-founder of The National Trust, with next-door Springfold, which has a notable garden occasionally open to the public. The road curves sharply to the left and you ignore a footpath turning on the right. The road curves left again and you pass a sign indicating that you are back in Haslemere. It then straightens and you pass St Ives, a preparatory school for girls. Passing a turning coming in from the right, continue on until you turn sharply right. You pass another turning on the right, Kemnor Park, and later join a footpath on the left taking you to the A286 main road. A sign on the left indicates that on this site formerly stood the Haslemere Manor House, built in 1827 and demolished for road improvements in 1928.

6 Cross the road and turn left along the pavement. You will soon see the Haslemere Museum on the left. This is well worth a visit.

Opposite the museum is The Town House, once the home of the Rev James Fielding who for some time was suspected of also being a highwayman. After his death a cache of 18th-century mail bags was discovered under the floorboards. Re-cross the road and continue back to the pub.

Brook
The Dog and Pheasant

The Dog and Pheasant is in the hamlet of Brook, which has a namesake in another part of the county, near Albury. This Brook has a distinctive 6-acre cricket ground opposite the pub, just over the village green. The ground, together with the smart building which provides a pavilion and village hall, was presented to the locality by the late Viscount Pirrie in 1923 and bears his name.

The pub was originally a medieval hall house and is thought to date from the latter half of the 15th century. Attractively beamed, this smart hostelry, with its shiny tables and comfortable seating, enjoys the patronage of a faithful clientele, comprising locals and many people from outside the village. All may expect a warm welcome.

Although not a large pub the kitchen has much to offer. The bar snacks menu is comprehensive and includes giant granary baps, ploughman's lunches and filled jacket potatoes. Listed on the main blackboard are the six or more daily specials, which change all the time, the majority being home-cooked. If you have room for more, there are puddings plus such things as ice-cream and cheese and biscuits, on a smaller board. The regular real ales are Tetley, Friary and Burton, and the guest ale changes every fortnight.

The pub is open on Monday to Friday from 12 noon to 2.30 pm and 5.30 pm to 11 pm, on Saturday from 12 noon to 3 pm and 6 pm to 11 pm, and on Sunday from 12 noon to 3 pm and 7 pm to 10.30 pm. Food is served on Monday to Friday from 12 noon to 2.15 pm and 7 pm to 9.30 pm, on Saturday from 12 noon to 2.30 pm and 7 pm to 9.30 pm, and on Sunday from 12 noon to 2.15 pm and 7 pm to 9.15 pm.

Telephone: 01428 682763.

How to get there: The pub is located in the hamlet of Brook, on the A286 between Godalming and Haslemere, opposite a large green.

Parking: The pub's car park is not large but, with permission, you are welcome to use it whilst on your walk. If it is full there are plenty of parking opportunities around the green opposite the pub.

Length of the walk: The walk is about 3 miles but this may be reduced by ½ mile if desired. OS maps: Landranger 186 or Pathfinder 1245 (inn GR 930380).

Commencing from Brook, the route takes you to the neighbouring hamlet of Sandhills and provides the opportunity to visit a sanctuary which is home to 150 donkeys as well as many other animals. Although short stretches of the popular Greensand Way are used you will discover that many of the paths are rarely trodden and you probably have them all to yourself.

The Walk

1 From the pub cross the main road to the green opposite and on the other side take a tarred track between the cricket ground and a pretty, walled garden. Pass Pirrie Hall on your left and continue onto a footpath under trees. You reach a road and turn left for about 250 yards to find a footpath fingerpost on your left. Turn left, passing the sign for 'Banacle Field', and go under trees, following a wire garden fence on your right. Bear right and join a path going up a slope and into woods. At the top of the slope you reach a T-junction.

2 Turn right onto a path forming part of the Greensand Way. The path becomes enclosed and later some steps lead you into a lane. Turn left and ignore an immediate turning on your right, thus leaving the Greensand Way, and pass The Hill House. Continue along the lane for about ½ mile, ignoring a footpath on the left as you turn sharply right. Shortly after passing Winkford Farm Cottages look for a sharp, hairpin turning on the right by a metal post.

3 Take the sunken, downhill bridleway, later ignoring a turning on the left by a gate. Continue downhill, passing two more left turns and

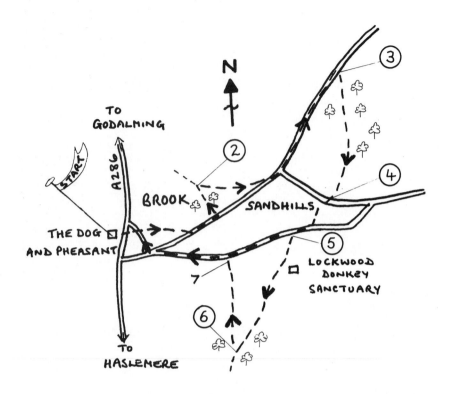

a field on your right. Keep to this track for almost ½ mile and reach
a driveway by Woodberry Cottage, which leads out to a lane.

4 Cross the lane to the public footpath opposite and rejoin the
Greensand Way, but only for a few yards. You pass a seat from where
there are better views in winter when the trees are leafless. The
Greensand Way plunges down to the left but you continue straight
ahead, going downhill on a narrow path. Turn right onto a track
heading towards a telephone box and come out to a road. Turn
right for a few yards where you will find a sign for the 'Lockwood
Donkey Sanctuary'. If you want to reduce the walk by about ½ mile
continue on the road for ¼ mile to reach point 7. But by going this
way you will not see the donkeys!

5 Turn left on the public bridleway and shortly reach the home for
donkeys founded by Mrs Kay Lockwood. I suggest you take some time
out of your walk to visit the sanctuary, particularly if you have
children in tow.

   To proceed with the walk, return to the track and turn left. In

Pirrie Hall, Brook.

another ¼ mile the main track turns left and another continues straight ahead but you take neither.

6 Turn sharply right on an un-signposted footpath but where a right of way does exist. Go over a ditch, scramble up a bank and follow a wire fence on your left on what may be an overgrown and brambly path for a short stretch. However, if you follow the fence you should not have any difficulty in finding your way. You reach the remains of a stile and go over a small concrete footbridge into a field. Keep close to the wood on your right and when this ends maintain direction straight across the field. Aim to pass to the left of a small copse and on towards a gate and stile immediately to the right of an evergreen hedge surrounding a house and garden. If the field is covered in corn or another crop you should find a convenient gap through it going pretty well straight up the field. As the fingerpost by the stile/gate indicates, a right of way does exist across it.

7 You come out onto a road and turn left past the Tudor-styled Meadow Cottage. With care, continue along the road as it curves right then left and after about ¼ mile reach a turning on the right signposted to Milford and Godalming. Take this road, ignoring an immediate turning on the right, and shortly you will be back at the green you crossed at the beginning of the walk. Turn left back to the pub.

4 Pirbright
The Cricketers

The Cricketers has an attractive setting overlooking a large duck pond, with an expansive green beyond. Pirbright is an historic village with a great military connection and was the home of one of the world's most famous journalists who went in search of one of its greatest explorers.

This is a fairly small pub, comfortable and cosy, with friendly and efficient service. It is family run and the landlord, who moved in at the age of three, looks set to stay. Part of the building dates back to the 16th century and the beamed ceilings made of a ship's timbers provide evidence of this. Folklore has it that England's last bare-fisted prize fighter was arrested here. The pub has a large garden which is packed on sunny weekend lunchtimes, so try to arrive early. Swings and slides are there for the children's enjoyment and dogs are also allowed in the garden, but not inside the pub. Although there is not a family room as such there is a games room with some dining tables which accompanied children are welcome to use. However, you are advised to check their availability before ordering.

The regular menu contains a good range of typical pub food. Choices include fish, chicken, omelettes, salads, burgers, ploughman's lunches, sandwiches (toasted or otherwise) and children's favourites. The specials board usually has three or four main dishes, the beef in Guinness pie and pork with cider always proving popular. Also on offer, but only when good specimens are available, are baked potatoes with a range of fillings. The real ale regulars are Tetley and London Pride and there are always one or two guest ales to consider. Dry Blackthorn cider comes through a pump and draught Guinness is also dispensed. Wine is available by the bottle or glass.

The pub is open on Monday to Friday from 12 noon to 2.30 pm and 6 pm to 11 pm, on Saturday from 11 am to 11 pm and on Sunday from 12 noon to 3 pm and 7 pm to 10.30 pm. Food is served every day from 12 noon to 2 pm, and on Friday and Saturday only between 7 pm and 9 pm.

Telephone: 01483 473198.

How to get there: Pirbright is south-west of Woking and north-west of Guildford. The A324 passes through the village and the pub is easily located facing onto the large green, with the pond immediately in front.

Parking: The pub's car park is in front and you are welcome to use it whilst on the walk, but please seek permission and ensure that you are not blocking any important goods entrances. Additional parking around the green is also usually available.

Length of the walk: 2½ miles. OS maps: Landranger 186 or Pathfinder 1205 (inn GR 947559).

Although you are close to a large area of military activity little of this will be in evidence, apart from, perhaps, the sound of an NCO barking encouragement to a platoon of squaddies. In the main the paths take you through tranquil conifer woods and along tracks through heather and gorse, ablaze with colour in summer. There will also be the chance to see the gravestone of Henry Morton Stanley.

The Walk

1 From the pub turn immediately right on a public footpath which commences as a tarred driveway. Later bear left as the driveway enters a nursery. Your path turns sharp right past some greenhouses and continues through conifer plantations. Later continue on a pleasant woodland path taking you on towards a sleeper bridge and stile which you cross over into a field. Bear diagonally right across the field to its corner, crossing another stile to reach White's Farm, with its attractive beams, and a T-junction.

2 Turn left, shortly bearing right as you reach a farm gate. Go past

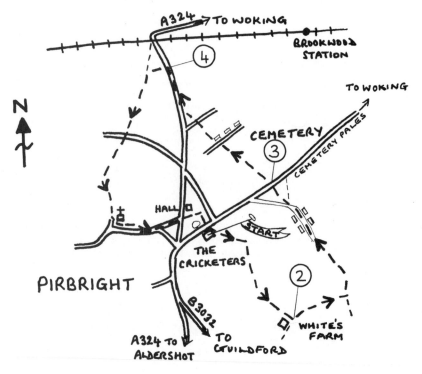

a barn, continuing along a footpath which later leads you past some houses to a T-junction. Turn left along a country lane which later becomes a residential road and, after about ¼ mile, you will find it curving left. Here, ignore a footpath on the right and continue another 25 yards to join a bridleway which is marked by two short posts, also on the right. Continue on the narrow path across this pleasant area of heather, gorse, pine and birch and reach a road. The road has the strange name of Cemetery Pales and it divides the huge Brookwood Cemetery in two.

The cemetery was originally opened as a last resting place for the deceased of London as graveyard space gradually ran out in the capital. For some time it even had its own station and railway branch line, on which travelled 'coffin trains' from Waterloo where there was a special platform. In this massive cemetery there were large separated areas for Catholics and Anglicans and, more recently, Muslims have been allocated considerable space, too. The area also houses a large military cemetery for fallen Commonwealth, American and other allied servicemen of World War II.

3 Cross the road, with care, to join the bridleway which continues

White's Farm, Pirbright.

opposite. After walking for about ¼ mile along this lovely path, which includes no less than four sleeper bridges, you reach a small residential road. Cross over to join a footpath opposite. Maintain direction over a crossing track and later come out to a very straight roadway which leads to Brookwood Cemetery. Cross the roadway and continue on a path opposite, which runs parallel with the road on the left. When you notice the last of a row of houses (a white one – 'Broadview'), leave the path at a fingerpost to join the road, which you should cross with care. Turn right and shortly you pass Caterham Close (a reminder of another Guards' Depot) then, just beyond, seek a little path on the left.

4 Turn left on this footpath, with a garden fence on your left, and shortly reach a T-junction with a fingerpost. Turn left and continue on this woodland path for about ¼ mile where you will reach another road. Cross the road to the enclosed footpath opposite, which winds its way between fields and in another ¼ mile reaches St Michael's church. Go through a little gate into the churchyard, passing the church on your left.

The church is one of the few Georgian places of worship in the diocese but its history goes back to the 13th century. The attractive tower is built of sarsen stone capped with a lead-sheathed spire. Just before the war memorial, and where the path leads to a gate and a road, look to your left for the large granite block forming the gravestone dedicated to Henry Morton Stanley and members of his family. Stanley and his famous 'Dr Livingstone, I presume' is something even the weakest member of the History class will recall. In 1871 he was sent by his employer, the editor of the *New York Times*, to find the great explorer in deepest Tanganyika. Stanley was born a Welshman but became an American. Eventually, the former soldier, journalist and explorer returned to Britain, where he was knighted and elected an MP. Finally, he settled in Pirbright at Furze Hill.

Leave the churchyard by the nearby gate and turn left along the road, later bearing left to reach the main road. Cross over to join a path running across the green. On your left you have the village hall which was given in 1899 to the parish by Lord Pirbright, who lived at Henley Park. This was originally a mansion but now forms part of a factory a mile or two south of the village. Two years earlier, to mark Queen Victoria's Diamond Jubilee, he presented the village with its first drinking fountain. On your right you will have a close view of the village pond. Beyond the pond you will find another path which will take you straight over to the pub.

5 Chobham
The Four Horseshoes

The Four Horseshoes enjoys a prominent position overlooking a green beyond which lies Chobham Common. It is in the small district of Burrowhill, ½ a mile north of the village of Chobham itself. Although the walk does not go through the village it is well worth a visit. Despite its growth over the years and proximity to motorways and the densely populated areas of Surrey, it has managed to preserve its character. A short walk along the High Street will allow you to enjoy some of its historic architecture, including the handsome parish church of St Lawrence dating from 1080.

No one, including the pub's owners, Courage Breweries, seems to be able to throw any light on its origins or history. Nevertheless, its shape and construction suggest considerable antiquity. Apparently, at one time the cellar was used as a mortuary, so it doesn't take too many guesses as to where this pub's ghost lives. Inside, the low oak-beamed ceilings and general atmosphere suggest an inn going back a century or two or even more. The tiny snug bar is most attractive and is very popular with the village regulars. Children are allowed in the pub but dogs are confined to the snug only.

The specials board always has three or four choices and one that

25

took my eye was the steamed bacon suet pudding served with parsley sauce, new potatoes and vegetables. The landlord cooks the ham and many of the other dishes. Everything available, apart from sandwiches, is shown on a blackboard. Options include vegetarian dishes and favourites such as jacket potatoes, ploughman's lunches and lasagnes. Children's portions are offered. Otherwise, helpings are generous. The regular real ale is Courage Best and there are always two guest ales, which are changed fortnightly from a range of about fourteen. The draught cider is Dry Blackthorn and, besides an extensive wine list, house wines are served by the bottle or glass.

The pub is open on Monday to Saturday from 11 am to 3 pm and 5.30 pm to 11 pm, and on Sunday from 12 noon to 3 pm and 7 pm to 10.30 pm. Food is served every day from 12 noon to 2.15 pm and, on Tuesday to Saturday, from 7.30 pm to 9.30 pm.

Telephone: 01276 857581.

How to get there: The pub is just off the B383 Sunningdale road, north of Chobham village. Leave the M3 at junction 3 and take the A322 and A319 or, if coming from the Woking direction, the A3046 to Chobham.

Parking: There is a car park behind the pub which, with permission, you are welcome to use whilst on the walk. Additional parking will be found on the little roads leading across the green to the pub.

Length of the walk: 3 miles. OS maps: Landranger 186 or Pathfinder 1189 (inn GR 970629).

Very soon you will find yourself on Chobham Common, little of which is enclosed. It has earned national recognition as one of the finest examples of lowland heath in Europe. Apart from its fairly recent dissection by the M3 and the majestic pylons, the common remains essentially the same as it has for hundreds of years.

The Walk

1 Facing away from the pub, go ahead towards an old water pump, cross the road and turn left for a few yards. Turn right on Gorse Lane. Ignore a left and then a right fork, continuing on the tarmac. As the roadway bears right towards some works continue straight ahead on a bridleway under trees. Go between two wooden posts and then fork right, soon ignoring another right fork. Continuing straight ahead, you should be able to see a field through the trees on the left. Go over a crossing track at a post and, about 100 yards or so after going under power cables, reach a crossing track.

26

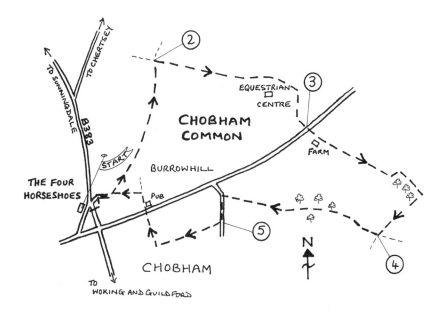

Chobham Common is home to a variety of wildlife and is steeped in history. Elsewhere on the common, but not passed on the walk, is an obelisk commemorating the visit by Queen Victoria in 1853 to review the troops who then occupied much of this area.

2   At the crossing track turn right towards a post, soon passing a seat on your left. Keep right at a fork. You pass under the power cables again where you ignore a small left fork and bear round to the right. Ignore another left fork and reach a crossing track where you continue ahead on a narrow path, with a ditch on your left. Soon turn left to join a main track coming in from the right and continue, with a large equestrian area over on your right. Go over a footbridge, ignore a fork on the left and continue ahead, shortly bearing right. You reach a crossing track and turn right, continuing over the next crossing track to arrive at a roadway. Turn left, immediately ignoring a right fork, and reach a road.

3   Cross the road onto a footpath forming the driveway to Rambridge Farm. As the driveway bears right to the farm, go straight ahead over a stile onto a path running between electric fences. Climb another stile between gates and continue straight ahead, following the direction of the fingerpost. Cross a sleeper bridge and turn left towards a post. Here you turn right through a gate and continue along the edge of a field and woods. At the end of the woods turn sharply right, soon

27

Cannon commemorating Queen Victoria's visit to Chobham.

going over a stile and shortly over another. Continue across a field, with a fence on your right. The next stile leads you onto a farm track and you reach a four-way fingerpost.

4 Turn right over a stile and cross a paddock diagonally left, to another stile and a bridge. Turn right through a metal gate, cross another paddock, with a ditch on your right, and go over (or under!) a stile onto a pleasant woodland path. Eventually, your path becomes a metalled driveway and you maintain direction to come out to a road. Cross the road and turn left for 100 yards or so, reaching a public bridleway fingerpost on the right.

5 Turn right on the bridleway and later cross a brick bridge. You come out onto an unmade roadway and, after a few yards, turn right on a footpath with a fingerpost. Continue through a metal barrier onto Red Lion Lane and shortly continue between houses, soon reaching a tarred road. Cross over, passing the Red Lion pub on your right, and go over a roadway to join footpath no 49. At the top of the slope you reach a T-junction and turn left, then right, passing Killy Hill cottages. Continue straight ahead, ignoring branching paths, and shortly reach a road where you bear left to retrace your steps back to the pub.

Horsell Common
The Bleak House

The Bleak House, folklore claims, acquired its name around 150 years ago due to its lonely position. At that time it was located in an isolated, bleak spot and locals suggested it would never do well. Mind you, the pub seemed to have plenty of customers, judging by the photograph of staff and regulars above the fireplace. They look as contented as any one could in the hard times of the latter part of the 19th century. Today, the pub trades on its Dickens' connection and, fronting onto one of the arteries leading to the M25, is in an extremely busy position. Also, far from being bleak, it's a warm, comfortable and friendly house. Although as recently as the 1960s it was a tiny country inn, since then, like Topsy, it has 'grow'd' – but is still not so large as to be impersonal.

The landlord is also chef and offers an excellent range of good food. There are Sunday roasts, steaks and many other choices, with sandwiches and baguettes for the less hungry. A real 'Dickens of a Dinner' at a bargain price is achievable if you eat early on a Monday to Saturday evening or throughout Sunday lunchtimes. If you don't already experience 'Monday blues' you can easily do so here, but in a pleasant way. In the musical sense Monday is 'Blues Night', but if

29

your preference is Classic Rock arrange your visit on a Thursday evening instead. The regular beers coming from the pumps are Tetley, Burton and Friary and the guest ale changes weekly. You will also find Olde English cider and draught Guinness.

The pub is open on Monday to Friday from 11 am to 3 pm and 5.30 pm to 11 pm, on Saturday from 11 am to 3 pm and 6 pm to 11 pm, and on Sunday from 12 noon to 3 pm and 7 pm to 10.30 pm. Food is served on Monday to Friday from 12 noon to 2.30 pm and 5.30 pm to 9.30 pm, on Saturday from 12 noon to 2.30 pm and 6 pm to 9.30 pm, and on Sunday from 12 noon to 2.30 pm – no food in the evening.

Telephone: 01483 760717.

How to get there: From the Six Cross Roads roundabout, north of Woking, take the A320, signposted to Chertsey and the M25 (at junction 11). The pub is a little less than ½ mile away on the right, but indicate early as this is a very busy road.

Parking: The pub has a reasonably large car park, which extends right into the common, and you do not need to seek permission to use it. Alternatively, there is another car park, much used by dog walkers, on the other side of the road. The entrance to this is another 100 yards north of the pub, by a telephone box. Continue past some houses and go straight on for another 100 yards or so.

Length of the walk: 3 ½ miles. OS maps: Landranger 186 or Pathfinder 1190 (inn GR 016610).

This route takes you through the woodland and across the heathland of Horsell Common, a wonderfully wild and large piece of open space on the doorstep of Woking, one of Surrey's most heavily-populated towns. You will pass the very spot that HG Wells had in mind for the landing of the Martians in his book, 'The War of the Worlds'. You also go around the perimeter of Fairoaks Airport, from where you are more than likely to see a light aircraft landing or taking off. The walk concludes by crossing farmland before re-entering the woods.

The Walk

1 From the pub turn right and (with great care!) cross the road. In a few yards, at a metal public footpath sign and Thimble Cottage, turn left on a rough lane. When the lane turns sharply right continue ahead through posts into woods. When you meet a main track turn left through a car parking area (your alternative to the one at the pub) and go past a large metal gate. Shortly, you will come to a large, open, sandy area on your left. This is the spot HG Wells had in mind for the

30

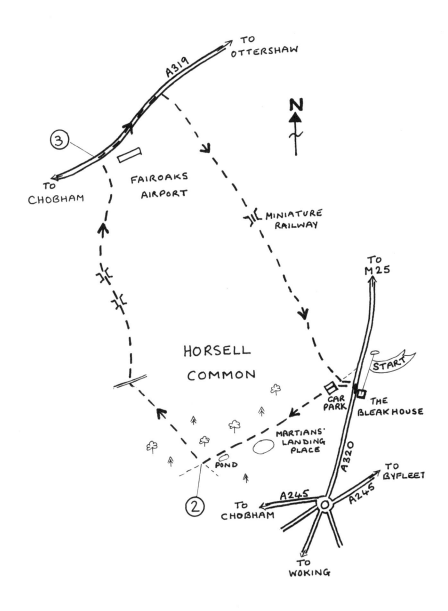

TO OTTERSHAW

A319

③

TO CHOBHAM

FAIROAKS AIRPORT

N

MINIATURE RAILWAY

TO M25

HORSELL COMMON

START

CAR PARK

THE BLEAK HOUSE

MARTIANS' LANDING PLACE

POND

②

A320

TO BYFLEET

A245

TO CHOBHAM

A245

TO WOKING

Site of the Martians' landing in 'War of the Worlds' on Horsell Common.

landing of the Martians' spacecraft, and the crater it formed. Wells was living in nearby Woking when he wrote *The War of the Worlds*. Many other landmarks and buildings in the locality are mentioned, too.

Soon after passing the open area, which had a lake until a few years ago, you will find a new lake, also on your left, which has only formed in the past few years. About 150 yards beyond you should discover a definite crossing track, easily discerned but, without your attention, quite easily missed, too.

2 Turn right into the woods on the narrow, sandy track and maintain direction, ignoring several branching paths and crossing tracks.

You now should be seeing Horsell Common at it wildest and most beautiful. Since 1910 it has been in the care of the Horsell Common Preservation Society. The society has subsequently secured the freehold.

You will not lose your way if you keep to this path, following it for almost ½ mile in a mainly north-westerly direction until it reaches an unmade roadway. Cross to a little path opposite and immediately join a signposted bridleway, on which you bear right. Continue in the same direction, with a field on your left, and, after passing a house on your right, the path bears left and then continues along the right side of a field. You are led across a bridge and through a gate and maintain direction across a field towards a public footpath signpost. By now you will easily be able to see Fairoaks Airport over on your right. Another gate and bridge lead you across the river again and you continue your northerly direction. As you get closer to the airport buildings your path becomes well-defined and later evolves into a roadway leading you out to a main road by the airport's west entrance.

3   Turn right along the road to pass the main entrance of the airport. The airport was originally built as a flying club field before the Second World War and was mainly patronised by the London Passenger Transport Board Flying Club. During the war it was used for manufacturing and storage by Vickers of Weybridge. Later it once again became a private flying field for trainers and recreational flyers. It is now a very busy commercial enterprise with executive and other small aircraft regularly taking off and landing all day long. After passing the end of the perimeter fence and a field on your right, turn right on a roadway (Bonsey's Lane), signposted as a public footpath. Later the roadway bears left but you keep ahead on a path which eventually leads you very close to the airport runway (be ready to duck if necessary!) and over a bridge. As you reach the buildings of a large nursery on the left you should look over the fence. Here you will not only discover a miniature railway but also a full-size station, complete with all the paraphernalia imaginable (the railway is open to the public on weekends via Mizen's farm shop on the A320). Your path merges with a concreted farm track and goes across a field. After passing a house on your right maintain direction along a roadway and you will soon reach a crossing track. Continue straight ahead for the pub or turn right for the car park on the common.

Sutton Green
The Fox and Hounds

The Fox and Hounds is, by Surrey village standards, relatively new and was built on the site of a former inn during the first decade of the 20th century. The pub was traditionally the meeting place for the Sutton Fair Day held on 1st May and, as its name would hint, also of the Hunt Supper. Today, it is a most pleasant inn with attractive decor, especially in the dining area. There is a comfortable feel about the place, welcoming staff and not-too-obtrusive background music.

Most landlords claim it would not pay them to home-cook their desserts. Well, here it has been proved otherwise. If you don't believe me, try the very special banoffi pie or any of the other mouth-watering choices. Everything, but everything, is home-made. The usual favourites, such as jacket potatoes, salads, ploughman's lunches, home-made soups, sandwiches and rolls, as well as steaks, are always available. The frequently changing specials include such things as lamb goulash, chicken and ham pie and many more, all listed on three separate blackboards. The full menu is available every lunchtime and evening. The real ales are the Ind Coope regulars, Burton, Tetley and Friary, the cider is Olde English and house wines are available by the bottle or glass. Children are permitted in the restaurant and special

34

children's meals are available. They are, of course, also welcome in the garden. Although well-behaved dogs may accompany their owners there, too, they are not allowed inside the building.

The pub is open on Monday to Friday from 11 am to 3 pm and 5.30 pm to 11 pm, on Saturday from 11 am to 3 pm and 6 pm to 11 pm and on Sunday from 12 noon to 3 pm and 7 pm to 10.30 pm. Food is served all week from 12 noon to 2 pm and 7 pm to 9 pm. Telephone: 01483 772289.

How to get there: The village lies between Woking and Guildford. If coming from either town leave the A320 on the turning signposted to 'Sutton Green'. Turn into Sutton Green Road and the pub will be found on the left at the junction with New Lane. If using the A3 (London to Portsmouth road), take the Merrow/Burpham exit. Go over the roundabout, right at the second roundabout and then follow the signs for 'Jacobs Well' and 'Sutton Green'.

Parking: The pub has a large car park which you are welcome to use whilst on the walk, but please let the staff know.

Length of the walk: 3½ miles. OS maps: Landranger 186 or Pathfinder 1206 (inn GR 005544).

Not far from this route stands that most opulent of mansions, Sutton Place, built by Sir Richard Weston in 1523, after he had received the manor of Sutton from Henry VIII in recognition of his diplomatic skills in France. The third Sir Richard Weston built the nearby Wey Navigation, which you follow for part of the walk. Although you are so near to two of the county's largest towns, there is a true feel of the countryside and it is only the occasional glimpse of a Woking office tower that reminds you of the close proximity of urban Surrey.

The Walk

1 From the pub cross the road, turn left and, at the road junction, continue straight ahead, still on Sutton Green Road. On the left look for a white house, The Old Post Office. Originally a 16th century smoke bay house, it was recorded as a shop and post office in the 19th century and restored this century. In about ¼ mile, after the last house on the right, turn right on a public footpath, also leading to Holfords Special Works Ltd. Almost immediately go over a stile by a gate and cross the next stile into Wareham's Farm yard passing disused barns and cattle pens on your left. With two farm gates in front of you bear left, following the direction of a fingerpost, onto a potentially boggy path which eventually reaches a bridge over the Wey Navigation.

If you turned right you would soon be walking alongside the

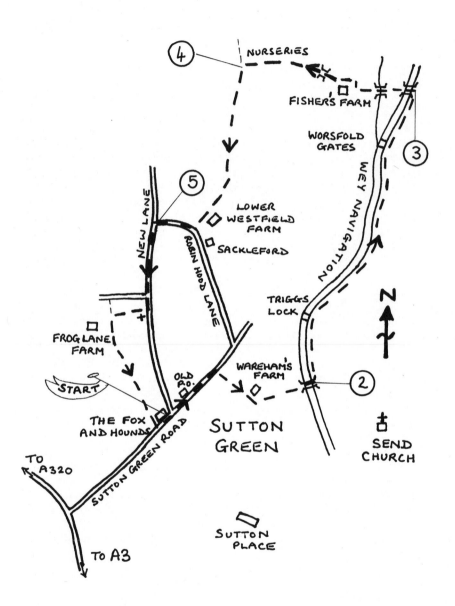

NURSERIES

④

FISHER'S FARM

WORSFOLD GATES

WEY NAVIGATION

③

⑤

NEW LANE

ROBIN HOOD LANE

LOWER WESTFIELD FARM

SACKLEFORD

TRIGGS LOCK

N

FROG LANE FARM

START

OLD P.O.

WAREHAMS FARM

②

THE FOX AND HOUNDS

SUTTON GREEN

SEND CHURCH

TO A320

SUTTON GREEN ROAD

TO A3

SUTTON PLACE

The Old Post Office, Sutton Green.

grounds of Sutton Place, which may be seen in part from the Wey but only closely viewed when visited by prior arrangement. In recent years Sutton Place has been in the ownership of three different American oil magnates, including Paul Getty.

2 However, for the purposes of our walk we turn left, when over the bridge, along the towpath of the Wey Navigation, which was begun in 1651 by a former owner of Sutton Place, the third Sir Richard Weston. Running from the Thames at Weybridge, it is navigable for the 19 miles to Godalming. On the right we are close to hilly country, part of the North Weald. If you look closely across the meadows, which are often flooded in winter, you should be able to make out the tower of Send church.

Shortly pass Triggs Lock, one of 16 – containing a total of 64 gates – on the Navigation, and go over a footbridge. Continue along the towpath, which curves left and then right and takes you over another bridge. A footpath leads off to the right but you continue ahead to pass through Worsfold flood gates where the river Wey joins the Wey Navigation. In another ¼ mile reach a metal footbridge.

3 Cross the bridge and continue straight ahead. Having crossed the Wey Navigation you now cross the river Wey via another bridge. You reach a gate leading to a house, Fisher's Farm, and turn right over a stile. Immediately turn left and go straight across a field, heading for a footbridge on the other side. The office tower in central Woking is well in view on the skyline over on your right. Once over the bridge use two stiles taking you over a farm track and continue ahead on a narrow, enclosed path past a nursery on your right until you reach a narrow roadway.

4 Turn left past a house and go over a stile by a gate into a field, keeping along the right side. Cross a stile by a gate, then another stile and a field. Go over a sleeper bridge and stile, following the fence on your left. You cross a barrier and continue towards the buildings of Lower Westfield Farm, which you pass on your left. Cross a stile and bear left into trees and reach Robin Hood Lane, which was once called Crookedidiliums Lane.

Sutton Green's other pub, the Bold Robin Hood, was just along to the left here, now a white-painted private house, Sackleford, with a white picket fence.

To continue the walk turn right and you will shortly reach a junction with a road, New Lane.

5 Cross the road and turn left, in a ¼ mile passing a turning off to the right, Pyle Hill. Pass three more houses and then locate a footpath on the right just before reaching All Soul's church.

Turn right and in a little under 200 yards reach a T-junction and turn left by a kissing gate. Shortly, pass Frog Lane Farm, whose many fine beams are said to come from old ships' timbers. You join the tarred driveway leading away from the house and eventually reach the road with the pub on your left.

⑧ Guildford
The Jolly Farmer

There has been a pub on this site from the early part of the last century and on a wall inside hangs a picture showing how it looked at the beginning of this one. The present building dates from 1913 but in recent years the pub, in its splendid riverside setting, has undergone massive refurbishment. It has the feel of a ship, with an upper deck bar and a lower deck restaurant. Outside there is an open terrace.

The standard of cuisine is high and the choice excellent. Seven main dishes are available every day and specialities include beef in Guinness pie, lamb hot pot, steak in cheese, and chicken and mushrooms. Walkers' favourites such as ploughman's lunches, jacket potatoes and open sandwiches are well represented, there usually being five choices of each. The pub manager doubles as chef and loves preparing curry and rice dishes. When he is not too busy, straightforward grilled steaks are also on offer. Best of all, the prices are moderate and the helpings generous. The real ales are served in peak condition. The pub's regular threesome are Friary, Burton and Tetley, with Marston's Pedigree and Wadworth 6X alternating as the guest ales. Accompanied children are welcome everywhere, apart from the bar area, but dogs are not allowed on any part of the premises.

39

The pub is open on Monday to Saturday from 11 am to 11 pm, and on Sunday from 12 noon to 3 pm and 7 pm to 10.30 pm. Food is served on Monday to Saturday from 12 noon to 2.30 pm and 6 pm to 8 pm, and on Sunday from 12 noon to 2.30 pm and 7 pm to 8 pm. Telephone: 01483 38779.

How to get there: The pub can be found less than ½ mile from Guildford town centre on the A281 Horsham road.

Parking: The pub only has parking for a few cars and these spaces are usually taken, so it would be sensible to use the adjacent Millbrook car park. Here you need to 'Pay and Display' but parking is free in the evenings, and all day on Sundays.

Length of the walk: 4 miles. OS maps: Landranger 186 or Pathfinder 1225 (inn GR 997489).

You soon leave the bustle of Guildford on a pleasant towpath and walk along the winding river Wey, always attractive whatever the season. Before joining farmland paths you will come to an impressive chapel ruin in its lofty hillside setting and, later on, a stately mansion which has been in the same family for over four centuries.

The Walk

1   From the pub turn right along the main road and almost immediately use an iron footbridge taking you over the river Wey.

The Wey Navigation, in the care of the National Trust since 1968, runs 19 miles from the Thames at Weybridge to Godalming, where the river continues but is not navigable. It was completed in 1764 and commercial carrying continued until 1950. Since then the river has become increasingly popular with pleasure craft, with boats for hire and plenty of moorings for private owners.

To continue the walk, turn left along the riverbank, passing Guildford Rowing Club's boathouse on the other side, once a loading point for locally quarried chalk. Go over a sluice gate and continue along the towpath until you come to a North Downs Way (NDW) sign. Just ahead is a footbridge, which was opened in 1985 and connects the NDW at a spot where a ferry once operated. At this point the NDW follows the same route as the Pilgrims' Way, which runs from Winchester to Canterbury. Turn right, passing Chaucer's Spring. Shortly go over a railway bridge which is in between two tunnels, Sand Tunnel to the left and Chalk Tunnel to the right. Just before you reach the main road ahead turn left, go over a driveway and bear left up a slope to arrive at St Catherine's Chapel dating from 1317. You will find more information on a board. Retrace your steps down to the

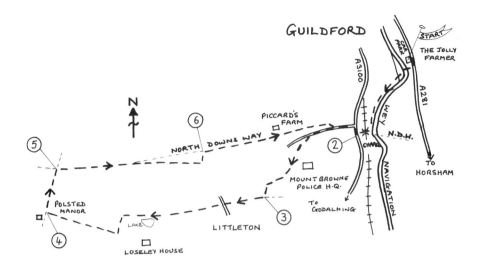

main road opposite the College of Law, which is on the site of the old Braboeuf Manor. The road is the old coaching route to Portsmouth, which was replaced this century by the A3, bypassing both Guildford and Godalming.

2 Turn right along the road for a few yards and, by the Olde Ship Inn, carefully cross over into Sandy Lane. Shortly you will notice that the NDW branches off to the right at the entrance to Piccard's Farm, which you will pass later, but you continue ahead. Where the pavement ends keep on the signposted public footpath, going uphill under trees. Gradually the path veers away from the road down on the right and you reach the top of the slope. Your path curves to the left and you pass a fingerpost incorrectly suggesting that the NDW, which you have already left, turns to the right. Continue ahead, cross a driveway leading to some houses (The Firs) and follow the direction of the next fingerpost. Shortly, over on your left, you will find the buildings of Mount Browne, the headquarters of the Surrey Police, and soon some good views may be glimpsed through the trees on your left. Your path narrows, is potentially overgrown, and curves left as you pass a police dog training complex and reach a T-junction.

3 Turn right along the side of a large field on your right. At a gate your path widens into a farm track and you pass a house on your left with an ornate car port. The path becomes tarred and you cross a road at Littleton, passing the former village school on your left. Cross a stile and go straight across a field. Cross another stile by a gate, ignore a left

41

St Catherine's Chapel, Guildford.

turn, and go straight over the next field to a stile to the left of a grand oak tree ahead. After crossing the stile maintain direction across the next field to another stile. Continue on a farm track and shortly an attractive lake comes into view.

Beyond is Loseley House, built of stone (from the ravaged Waverley Abbey) in the 1560s by Sir William More. It is still in the ownership of the same family, through marriage, the More-Molyneux. It is open for visits during the summer months. You can also go on a farm tour and the rare-breed sheep are likely to be the friendliest you have ever encountered. The estate's dairy farm produces a distinctive cream used in the famous Loseley ice-cream sold in Harrods Food Hall and other discerning outlets all across southern England.

Continuing the walk you cross a stile on your left. Maintain direction past a gate and cross another stile to continue along the left perimeter of the next field, soon turning left. In a few more yards go over a stile on the left and continue along a tree-lined path. You are led over another stile and out to a track by a tall fingerpost. Turn right along the wide track and shortly go through a normally open, white-painted barrier-gate by a house. Soon you will find some pig pens to your left and right, with the pigs running free in the fields. You reach a junction of paths, with Little Polsted ahead and Polsted Manor to your left.

4 Turn right on a gully-like path, soon ignoring a left turn, and continue ahead under trees. You will notice some more pig pens over on your right and shortly, on your left, you'll probably see the traffic speeding along the A3. Your path commences to climb and you reach a crossing track by a three-way fingerpost.

5 Turn right, back onto the NDW. A track comes in from the right (nature trail – not a right of way) and you continue ahead on a wide, sandy track, under trees but with occasional views over to your left. After about ¼ mile you fork left, following the acorn sign indicating the NDW, and then immediately turn right. In another ¼ mile you reach a T-junction and turn left, soon reaching another junction of paths.

6 Turn right and shortly pass through Piccard's Farm yard. In another ⅓ mile you come out to a road (Sandy Lane) on which you turn left. Retrace your steps back into Guildford by going down to the main road where you turn right and very shortly left, over the railway. Head for the river and then go left along its bank.

Merrow
The Horse and Groom

The Horse and Groom has a central position in Merrow, which, although virtually part of Guildford, is a separate village with its own jealously preserved identity. Merrow is perhaps best known for the Downs above it, which until Victorian times provided the setting for a famous race course and grandstand unequalled at that time.

The pub, according to the sign on its grand frontage, dates from 1615 but local historians refute this and suggest that, although there may have been a farmhouse on the site at that time, the present building is more likely to have been built in the 1650s. It's an imposing building and looks particularly impressive when floodlit at night. Perhaps signifying the changing of clientele over the years, it has previously been named the Running Horse and the Hare and Hounds.

As it is part of the Allied Lyons 'Big Steak' chain, you can always be assured of a hearty meal. Besides the steaks there are many familiar choices, including traditional fare, as well as vegetarian dishes and cold platters – ploughman's, countryman's and, for those of nautical persuasion, a trawlerman's. There are also hot and cold filled baguettes and jacket potatoes. Real ale lovers can choose between Tetley, Burton, Young's Special and Friary. Wines are described on the menu and can be ordered by the glass or bottle. Tea and coffee are also served. Children are, of course, welcome to accompany dining adults in the pub and they have their own menu. Dogs on leads are, too, allowed in the pub and there is a beer garden.

The pub is open on Monday to Saturday from 11 am to 11 pm, and on Sunday from 12 noon to 10.30 pm. (Note: to drink between 3 pm and 7 pm on Sundays you'll need to be eating, too.) Food is served on Monday to Thursday from 12 noon to 2.30 pm and 6 pm to 9.30 pm, on Friday and Saturday from 12 noon to 2.30 pm and 6 pm to 10 pm, and on Sunday from 12 noon to 9 pm.

Telephone: 01483 573161.

How to get there: The pub is situated on the A246 Leatherhead road, 2 miles east of Guildford.

Parking: The pub has plenty of parking, which you are welcome to use whilst on your walk – and there is no need to seek permission. If it should be full there is a small public car park right opposite.

Length of the walk: 3 miles. OS maps: Landranger 186 or Pathfinder 1206 (inn GR 028507).

Here is another walk without climbs! Most of the route is across the vast Clandon Estate, with its panoramic views. There is also the opportunity of visiting Clandon, a mansion in the care of the National Trust, with an interesting collection of porcelain, furniture and needlework.

The Walk

1 From the pub turn right and cross the road to see the church of St John the Evangelist.

The church dates from the 1150s and underwent extensive renovation a century and a half ago. In the churchyard look for the gravestone of a gentleman named Walter Broke who died in 1603, aged 107 years. Local legend claims he walked to London on his 100th birthday.

From the church cross the main road and turn right along the pavement. At the roundabout cross over Park Lane towards the ornate gates of Clandon Park. By the West Lodge (left) look for a fingerpost and join a footpath. Shortly go through a metal gate and your path joins a tarred driveway. Soon after, if you look carefully over to your right, you will be able to make out the red-brick Clandon House. The driveway becomes gravelled and you soon leave it at a fingerpost by bearing left onto a wide, grassy farm track. Ignore a left fork and keep straight ahead. You reach some trees and will soon discover a pond

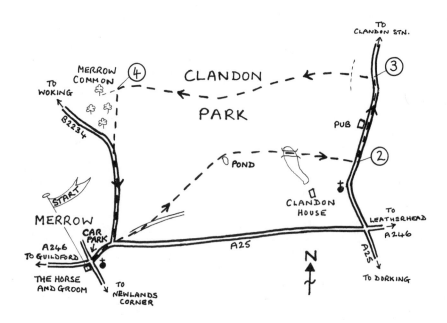

within them. Go over a track, passing a desolate farmyard on your right and, in a few yards, cross a waymarked stile. At the next waymark continue straight ahead over a track towards trees. Climb over a stile and shortly use a bridge to take you over a lake. Once over the next footbridge you will have a closer view of Clandon House.

To continue your walk, go over a crossing track and here you will have your closest view of the house. Follow the path ahead, soon coming out to a road.

If you wish to take some time away from your walk to visit Clandon House (NT) turn right for a few yards. If you proceed a little further down the road you will come to the church of St Peter and St Paul.

2 To continue your walk, turn left along West Clandon's meandering street. You will find an assortment of interesting houses, some quite ancient and others more recent, dating from the time when the opening of the station on the Waterloo – Guildford (via Cobham) line encouraged building for commuters. At one time the village bore the name of Clandon Regis and you will discover a fine house bearing this name over on your right. On your left you pass a busy pub, the Bull's Head, where a sign above the door says that a highwayman, Robert Newland, once slept here. After about ⅓ mile, just before a 'road narrows' sign, you'll find a stile on the left by a metal fingerpost.

46

The gates of Clandon Park, Merrow.

3 Turn left on the public footpath and cross a driveway, continuing on a grassy path under trees. Go over a farm track, over a stile and downhill on a tree-lined path. Cross another stile and the next way-mark directs you onto a footbridge over a gurgling stream. Follow along the side of a sloping field, keeping to the left perimeter. Go over a crossing track towards a clump of trees, still following along the side of this huge field. (Is it the largest in the whole county?) Your path curves to the left again and then continues in a straight line between fields towards the trees ahead.

4 You finally enter the woods of Merrow Common and immediately turn left on a narrow (permissive) path, shortly climbing over some fallen trees. Another path comes in from the right and you continue ahead, shortly entering a field. Keep to the left side of the field and then go under a barrier and out to a road by a roundabout. Bear left along the grass verge and, as you reach some houses on the right, carefully cross over the road to use the pavement on the other side. Eventually you reach the roundabout by the gates at the entrance to Clandon Park. Retrace your steps back to the pub or the car park opposite.

⑩ Ripley
The Talbot Hotel

The Talbot Hotel, built in the 17th century as a coaching inn, is situated on the old London – Portsmouth road in a picturesque location. Besides being an old coaching village, Ripley has been a popular venue for cricketers and cyclists since the last century. There are a number of listed period buildings and some antique shops which are well worth seeing.

This historic inn has retained its charm and character over the centuries and the resident ghost is reported to be quite benign. An imposing arched gateway leads to the old stable block where the resting horses were fed and watered. Inside are many of the original features, the traditional low-beamed bar giving a special feeling of antiquity. The bar is divided by a large fireplace, lit in winter, providing a comfortable, relaxed atmosphere. Besides the bars, there is a no smoking lounge and The Pantry restaurant from where all food may be ordered for delivery to whichever nook or cranny you chose to sit in. Outside are the terrace and garden areas where you can sit on sunny days in summer.

Most of the food is home-cooked and there are plenty of choices, including home-made pies and ranges of fish and salad dishes. Besides the regular menu there are daily changing specials, which may include such things as cheese, potato and onion bake, sweet and savoury crêpes and lasagne. The usual pub light meals such as soups and sandwiches are also available. Friary and Burton are the regular real ales and there are usually two others. Olde English cider, draught Guinness and a good selection of wines are also on offer. Children are allowed in the restaurant area and lounge but dogs are confined to the bars – both, of course, may use the terrace and garden. This is a 3-star hotel and there are several extremely smart bedrooms.

The bars are open on Monday to Saturday from 11.30 am to 3 pm and 5.30 pm to 11 pm, and on Sunday from 12 noon to 3 pm and 7 pm to 10.30 pm. Food is served every day from 12 noon to 2 pm and 7 pm to 9.30 pm (no salads on Sunday evenings in winter). Telephone: 01483 225188.

How to get there: Ripley lies just off the A3 Portsmouth road, north-east of Guildford. If travelling on the M25, leave at junction 10 and proceed south on the A3. Come off at the first slip road, signed to the B2215 and Ripley. The hotel is on the left, almost immediately after you enter the village.

Parking: The hotel has a large car park which, with permission, you are welcome to use whilst on the walk. Additional free parking is available on the opposite side of the road, on the village green.

Length of the walk: 2 ½ miles. OS maps: Landranger 187 or Pathfinder 1206 (inn GR 056569).

This pleasant, short ramble takes you through gentle countryside close to the river Wey, with its colourful houseboats, and across the roaring water at Walsham flood gates. After the walk you could take a short stroll along Ripley High Street, with its interesting shops, antique and otherwise.

The Walk

1 From the inn cross the road immediately, passing between an antique shop and some cottages, towards a cricket green. Bear round to the right past the pavilion and then go left along the pitch. On reaching some mobile covers continue ahead, with the trees on your right, on a narrow, but discernible, path. Ripley Green is reputed to be the largest village green in the country. Maintain your northerly direction by going several crossing paths and in and out of the trees. Other paths come in from both left and right but you always keep the large green on your left and the densest area of trees to your right. At the end of the green, keep right at a fork and head for a

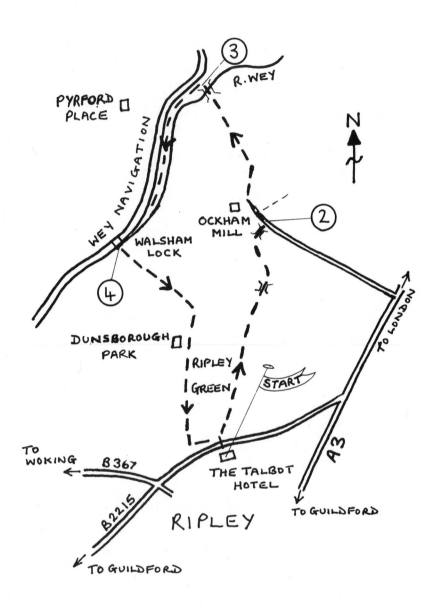

③

R. WEY

PYRFORD
PLACE

N

WEY NAVIGATION

OCKHAM
MILL

②

WALSHAM
LOCK

TO LONDON

④

DUNSBOROUGH
PARK

RIPLEY

GREEN

START

TO
WOKING

B367

A3

THE TALBOT
HOTEL

B2215

TO GUILDFORD

RIPLEY

TO GUILDFORD

The Walsham Lock on the river Wey, Ripley.

bridleway/footpath waymark leading you into woods. Soon you go over a footbridge and join what was once a byway, Holly Bush Lane, which is marked on a map dated 1769 as the old way from the village to Ockham Mill. You then go over another bridge and come out to a tarmac lane.

2 Turn left, soon ignoring a footpath leading off to the right, and walk towards Ockham Mill.

The mill was built in 1862 by the Earl of Lovelace. It is now a private residence but remains essentially the same as when it was built. There has been a mill on this site since 1297. Opposite is a half-timbered house, Millwater, with a lovely garden.

Once past the mill bear right onto an unmade track which soon curves left. Go over a wooden footbridge, then over another. The next footbridge, an extremely substantial one, takes you over the river Wey and very shortly to the Wey Navigation, which was begun in 1651 to link Guildford with the Thames and London.

3 Turn left along the towpath and shortly notice a large building close to the opposite bank, Pyrford Place. What was originally a 17th century mansion has now been converted into a luxurious apartment block. The imposing building with a domed roof served as a summer house for the former manor. After walking along this lovely stretch of the canal for a ½ mile or so you reach Walsham Lock and flood gates.

51

Here the Wey Navigation and the river go their separate ways, re-joining close to the river's mouth at Weybridge. You will notice that the lock is some 12-15 ft above the river.

4 Turn left over the weir and leave the canal by keeping straight ahead and shortly going over a footbridge next to a redundant stile. Having crossed another footbridge and passed another redundant stile and two white-painted houses, go over a brick bridge. Join a bridle-way and arrive back at Ripley's large green, turning right along a roadway and keeping the green to your left. When the roadway curves left keep straight ahead on a narrow path taking you past Dunsborough Park with its impressive topiary. The gardens here are open to the public on certain days of the year. Until her death the mansion was the home of the musical comedy actress of stage and screen, Florence Desmond. Shortly pass a children's play area with equipment, on your left, and as you reach the end of the green bear left, either along the green or the High Street, back to the inn.

Weybridge
The Lincoln Arms

The Lincoln Arms enjoys a waterside setting, close to the river Thames, a little way outside that epitome of Surrey's affluence, the pleasant town of Weybridge. The town's fame originates from the 16th century when Henry VIII built Oatlands Palace and started to attract visitors to what was then a tiny village at the confluence of the rivers Wey and Thames.

The pub was once a hunting lodge owned by the Earl of Lincoln and used by King Henry but commenced its life as two houses. How long it has been an inn does not seem to be documented but there is a photograph on the wall showing how it was in 1870 and it does not seem to have changed much since. It's a large place with plenty of seating, a busy atmosphere and background music. It is much patronised by young office workers on weekday lunchtimes and other people, some young and some just young-at-heart, in the evening and at weekends.

Almost all the food is home-cooked and the speciality is Tex-Mex, much appreciated by the large American community in the district, many of them suggesting it is the most authentic Mexican food they have tasted outside North America. The aim is for excellence and the landlord, who is also the head chef, loves to get as far away from normal pub grub as possible. There is a separate lunchtime and evening menu. The latter lays heavy emphasis on the Mexican food and there are steaks, a Thai speciality of stir fry with rice and spicy sauce, plus an interesting range of burgers. Some of the Mexican dishes may be available at lunchtime as well, along with more familiar food like baked potatoes, steak and ale pie, roast lamb and crusty rolls with the usual fillings. Vegetarians are catered for and children's portions are available. Desserts are offered but portions here are large and few diners have room for them. The regular, hand-pumped bitters are Burton and Tetley and the guest ale rotates monthly. The cider is Olde English and the house wine, served by the glass or bottle, is Australian. There are guest wines, too. Children are encouraged to sit in the family room, which is also a non-smoking area. There is a play area in the rear garden, with swings and climbing apparatus and so on. Dogs are allowed in the pub and in the gardens, front and back, but they must be kept on leads at all times.

The pub is open on Monday to Friday from 11.30 am to 2.30 pm and 5.30 pm to 11 pm, on Saturday from 11.30 am to 3 pm and 6 pm to 11 pm, and on Sunday from 12 noon to 3 pm and 7 pm to 10.30 pm. Food is served on Monday to Saturday from 12 noon to 2.30 pm and 6.30 pm to 9.30 pm, and on Sunday from 12 noon to 2.30 pm and 7.30 pm to 9.30 pm.

Telephone: 01932 842109.

How to get there: Weybridge is on the A317, between Chertsey and Esher. If approaching from the M25 (junction 11) take the A317 through Weybridge High Street and turn left at Monument Green. The pub is about a mile up Thames Street on the right-hand side, just before the road becomes Walton Lane.

Parking: The pub has a large car park which, with permission, you are welcome to use whilst on the walk. There is also a public car park by the riverside almost opposite the pub.

Length of the walk: 3 miles. OS maps: Landranger 176 or Pathfinder 1190 (inn GR 076656).

In a largely urban area, here is a little oasis in the form of a large island. The land close to the river Thames in Surrey is largely built up and very few 'country' circular walks are possible along its banks. I hope you enjoy this short walk which almost entirely follows the course of the river. On the opposite side are many enviable riverside properties with gardens leading down to the bank.

54

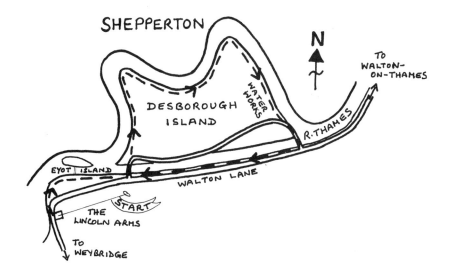

The Walk

From the pub cross the road and turn right, soon going under a barrier and across a car park to continue along the towpath, with the river on your left. You pass a footbridge leading to Eyot Island, the headquarters of the D'Oyly Carte Opera Company. Richard D'Oyly Carte (1844-1901) was a theatrical manager, famous as a producer of the Gilbert and Sullivan operas at the Savoy Theatre in London, which he built. Shortly, reach a bridge where you climb the steps leading up to a road and turn left over the bridge, opened in 1935, going across the river. Soon bear left through a gateway and then bear right along the riverbank once again, now on Desborough Island. The path swings about but you should keep as close to the riverbank as you can.

You will see several fine homes on the opposite side, some new and some pre-war, many owned by well-known personalities in the entertainment industry. Across the river is the pleasant town of Shepperton, famous for its film studios. Its postal address is Middlesex but as that county no longer exists as an administrative area it now forms part of the Surrey Borough of Spelthorne.

After a mile or so you will pass some rugby pitches on your right and beyond these join a roadway running along the side of reservoirs and waterworks buildings. You go between two 'no entry' road signs to a bridge similar to the one you crossed earlier. Cross to the other side and turn left down some steps, back to the river bank, and turn left. This section of the river Thames is a cut, built in the 1930s, to

River Thames at Weybridge.

shorten the route of the commercial river traffic, which previously used the meandering section that you walked along a little earlier. In a fraction over ½ mile you go under the bridge you crossed earlier. Retrace your steps along the towpath, noticing a bell used at displayed times for summoning the ferry across to Shepperton. Go through the car park, along the road, and back to the pub.

Wotton
The Wotton Hatch

The Wotton Hatch was at one time known as the Evelyn Arms honouring the name of the village's most famous son, the diarist John Evelyn, who was born at nearby Wotton House. Wotton means 'the farm by the wood' and Hatch is a 'gate', generally leading to a common. On the walls of this ornate inn are interesting pieces of memorabilia in the form of old photographs and pub invoices and so on. As well as the bar there is an elegant dining room in a conservatory and an enormous garden with plenty of tables and amusements for the children.

All the food, apart from desserts, is cooked on the premises and besides a comprehensive regular menu there are always about ten specials, which change daily. Along with all the normal pub favourites, such as grills and pies, there are vegetarian meals and, for the hungry walker on a budget, things like ploughman's lunches and sandwiches. You are welcome to call in just for a cup of coffee, if you wish. If you can make up a party of 20 or more you could order a special treat – a stir-fried meal cooked in the biggest frying pan in Surrey. It's 3 ft in diameter and weighs 120 pounds!

The real ales (all from Fuller's Griffin Brewery) are ESB, London

Pride and Chiswick. A regularly changing guest ale is drawn from the fourth pump. For cider drinkers there is Scrumpy Jack and you can order wine by the glass or bottle. Please note that children are welcome in any part of the pub, but dogs are only permitted in the little public bar and not in any of the areas where people eat.

The pub is open on Monday to Friday from 11 am to 2.30 pm and 6 pm to 11 pm, on Saturday from 11 am to 11 pm, and on Sunday from 12 noon to 3 pm and 7 pm to 10.30 pm. Food is served on Monday to Friday from 12 noon to 2.30 pm and 6.30 pm to 9.45 pm, on Saturday from 12 noon to 2.30 pm and 6.30 pm to 10 pm, and on Sunday from 12 noon to 2.30 pm and 7 pm to 9.45 pm.

Telephone: 01306 885665.

How to get there: The pub is very easy to find, being in a prominent position on the A25 between Guildford and Dorking, about 3 miles west of the latter, on the left.

Parking: The pub has a large car park which it shares with users of the village hall. You are welcome to use it whilst on your walk but be sure to let a member of staff know.

Length of the walk: 4½ miles. There is the option of reducing it to 2½ miles if you wish. OS maps: Landranger 187 or Pathfinder 1226 (inn GR 126476).

In no time you are well away from the busy A25 and enjoying a sweeping view across the valley, with the backdrop of the North Downs. Later you join a fine path along the side of a series of weirs forming lakes where trout abound.

This is a fine walk for a hot, sunny day as plenty of time is spent under the trees, and in autumn the shades of colour painted on the Downs' hillsides are quite spectacular but this is a lovely walk for all seasons.

The Walk

1 From the pub cross the A25, with care, and take the lane opposite, leading to the church of St John the Evangelist. Ignore a stile leading to a footpath on the right and continue down to the church.

This was the family church of the Evelyns and besides finding the brick mausoleum in the churchyard, remembering three generations of Evelyns, look for a headstone bearing the name of the composer Vaughan Williams. To rejoin the walk from the churchyard use the stile in the wall on the left.

If not entering the churchyard turn left over a stile and follow the right side of a field to find a stile in the church wall. Bear left across the field and go over a stile. Continue on the path running alongside

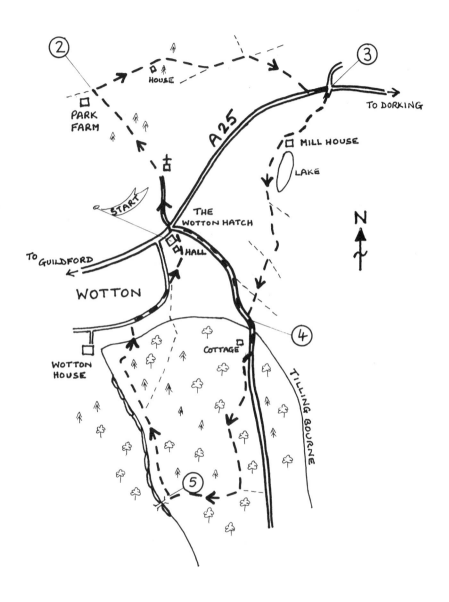

② PARK FARM

HOUSE

③ TO DORKING

A25

MILL HOUSE

LAKE

START

THE WOTTON HATCH

TO GUILDFORD

HALL

WOTTON

④

COTTAGE

WOTTON HOUSE

TILLING BOURNE

⑤

N

a wood and shortly enter the wood ahead. The path rises and then descends and you leave the woodland via a stile. Maintain direction across a field to another stile leading to a track by Park Farm.

2 Turn right on the bridleway, tarred at first, and in a little over ¼ mile pass a house. Continue under trees and, just before reaching a fence ahead, bear left through posts onto a narrow path which cuts a corner. Join another bridleway and, just beyond a left turning, turn right onto an enclosed footpath which later narrows between fences. You are brought out onto a driveway leading down to the A25 on which you should turn left. Cross the road with great care and continue to a turning on the right, Rookery Drive.

3 Turn right on the bridleway, part of the Greensand Way, which leads to houses, some new and some not so. The track curves to the right and on the left is the attractive Mill House with its bubbling waterfall.

Pass some new houses, The Rookery, on your right and bear left. As you travel along the bridleway, if you look to your left you should have frequent glimpses of the picturesque lake that feeds the waterfall you saw earlier. At a fork by a metal farm gate bear right on a footpath, still on the Greensand Way, and climb steeply. The path eventually levels out and takes you through posts to a crossing track. Go straight over the track and a parallel one to enter a field. Bear diagonally left across the field and reach a stile which you cross. Turn left for just a few yards and then right on an easily-missed, narrow path going under trees. Go over a tarred driveway and continue down the slope opposite to reach a lane.

For the shorter walk, turn right at this point, along the lane, and in ½ mile reach the pub.

4 *For the main walk*, turn left along the lane, soon crossing the Tilling Bourne and in 100 yards or so, just past Damphurst Cottage, turn right over a stile onto a narrow path which soon runs parallel with the lane below. Later the path curves away from the lane and, after climbing for several yards, flattens out. You will find a plantation on your right and you eventually reach a crossing track where you turn right. Later the track curves to the right and goes steeply downhill to a stile, taking you onto a crossing track with a brick bridge ahead.

5 You may like to go ahead for a few yards to see the ponds each side of the bridge, but to continue the walk turn right over a stile by a gate. As you trundle along this attractive path look to your left for the series of pools formed by weirs built by the Evelyns. In about ¼ mile do not be tempted to join an inviting path forking off to the right (although if you did it would eventually lead you back to the pub). Continue straight ahead, with the water feature still on your left. Later, just before the path curves to the right, look very carefully over to

St John the Evangelist church, Wotton.

your left and you should catch a glimpse of Wotton House. This was the home of generations of the Evelyn family from 1579.

Go over a crossing track to the path opposite, over a stile by the remains of a metal kissing gate, and across a field to another stile. After crossing the stile join a metalled driveway which leads, left, to Wotton House, but you turn right. At a 'Wotton Estate No Right of Way' sign leave the driveway by turning right over a stile into a field. Bear diagonally left across the field towards a wooden building, Wotton village hall, passing it on your left as you arrive back at the car park.

13 Ockley
The Old School House

The Old School House is situated on one of England's oldest roads, Stane Street. Its very straightness tells you it has to be a Roman road and when it was built, almost two millennia ago, it ran from the heart of old London town straight to Noviomagus, or Chichester as we know it today.

The pub was indeed once a school. A notice in the bar, dating from 1857, tells us the Ockley Commercial Boarding and Day Academy provided board and instruction at 18 guineas per annum for boys under twelve, 20 guineas for over-twelves and washing at two guineas per annum. Young boys were 'liberally boarded and carefully instructed'. Look on the wall for Robert Botting's letter to his parents dated December 1844. What a perfect little gentleman! Although the previous school house was thoroughly renovated, the old beams have been retained and the result is an extremely cosy and comfortable country pub.

Those who take eating out seriously will be delighted at what they find as everything here, including the mouth-watering puddings, is home-cooked. Nothing is bought in, so whether you use the regular bar menu or the specials board, usually offering about six interesting choices, you are in for a real treat. I tried 'Canadian Bison Casserole' and it was delicious. Examples of the puddings were orange mousse and shortbread and hot fruit strudel with custard. However, if your requirements are more modest, items such as home-made soup with crusty bread and appetizing sandwiches are available. The ales come up from the King and Barnes family-owned brewery in Horsham, in barrels marked 'Sussex', 'Broadwood' and 'Festive'. The draught cider is Stowford Press and there is an excellent selection of eight house wines sold by the bottle or glass. Dogs are permitted in the bar and children are welcome.

The pub is open on Monday to Saturday from 11 am to 3 pm and 6 pm to 11 pm (7 pm to 11 pm in winter) and on Sunday from 12 noon to 3 pm and 7 pm to 10.30 pm. Food is served on Monday to Saturday from 12 noon to 2.30 pm and 6.30 pm to 9.30 pm (7 pm to 9.30 pm in winter) and on Sunday from 12 noon to 3 pm and 7 pm to 9 pm. Telephone: 01306 627430.

How to get there: The pub is located on the A29 Bognor road at the south end of the village. Ockley lies south of Dorking and, if coming from that direction, leave the A24 at Beare Green for the A29 and travel another 3 miles.

Parking: You are welcome to use the pub's car park whilst on your walk, but please seek permission.

Length of the walk: 3 miles. OS maps: Landranger 187 or Pathfinders 1246 and 1226 (inn GR 145395).

This gentle walk is on mostly level ground, including some little-used paths offering frequent views of Leith Hill and its tower, the highest point in the south-east. An impressive view of Jayes Park mansion and its attractive lake comes early in the walk, which concludes by passing an extremely large duck pond.

The Walk
1   From the pub turn left along Stane Street. You pass another pub and many attractive cottages, some of them dating from the 17th century. After about ¼ mile you reach a large village green.

The green lies lower than the road, is ½ mile long, and is the spot where the Saxons fought and beat the Danes in AD 851, more than 200 years before the Battle of Hastings. Apparently, 'blood stood ankle deep' after the massacre.

Turn left on a small road, going between 30 mph signs, past a fine weather-boarded house and the village school dating from 1841. At the bottom of the road bear left at a fingerpost, shortly crossing a

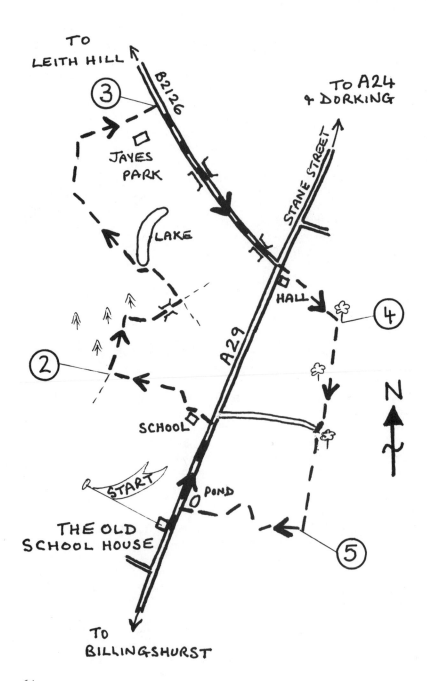

TO
LEITH HILL

③

B2126

TO A24
& DORKING

JAYES
PARK

STANE STREET

LAKE

②

A29

HALL

④

SCHOOL

N

START

POND

THE OLD
SCHOOL HOUSE

⑤

TO
BILLINGSHURST

16th & 17th century cottages at Ockley.

bridge and entering a graveyard. Immediately, bear right to a stile leading you into a field and then bear left across the field to its top left corner and a stile.

2 After crossing the stile turn right on a nicely surfaced bridleway running along the side of a wood, with fields on the right. The track takes a sharp right turn and eventually goes over a bridge and through a bridle gate into a field. Where the trees on the left end, turn sharp left and head for a footpath fingerpost ahead. There's a good view of Leith Hill and its tower here. At the fingerpost turn left, passing an attractive lake with Jayes Park mansion beyond. Go over a wooden bridge and stile and bear right up a field, heading for the left of the two gates at the top. You do not actually go through the gate but continue straight ahead on a concrete farm track, with cottages on the left. The track bears right towards farm buildings and when you reach a barn turn right through the farmyard. Continue on the driveway leading out of the farm and arrive at a road.

3 Turn right along the roadside, keeping well into the right, and go over Hatch Pond Bridge, continuing along the road to go over another bridge and along the side of the green. At the road junction cross over the A29 and take a footpath to the left of Ockley village hall. Bear diagonally right over a large field, which may be ploughed or in crop, but a right of way does exist across it in a south-easterly direction.

Head towards the top right corner but, close to the far side, you should find a path going into the trees about 50 yards to the left of the corner.

4 Enter a small copse and go over a stile, continuing straight across a field in a southerly direction, heading for the corner of a wood where you should find some waymarks. Continue straight ahead, keeping a fence on your right, and cross a stile. After crossing a second stile bear right into a wood, immediately bearing left and going over a metalled bridleway to a field gate. Continue down the left side of three fields, going through two more farm gates.

5 Turn right across the next field, going over a dry ditch and through a hedge opening into another field. Continue with a hedge on your right and, when this turns right, turn with it and follow the field boundary. Go right on a rough farm track, pass a large duck pond and arrive back at the A29 via a gate. Turn left across the road, back to the pub.

14 Newdigate
The Six Bells

The Six Bells, a freehouse located in the centre of a sleepy village, has been a pub for as long as records are available. Newdigate has many lovely old buildings and much of the village architecture dates from the 18th and 19th centuries, with several of the outlying farmhouses going further back into the 16th and 17th centuries.

The pub's name is derived from the number of bells in the church tower opposite. Prior to 1803 when the church had one bell less, it was called the Five Bells. Folklore suggests it was used as a 'safe house' for contraband and it is claimed that at one time a tunnel ran from the pub to the church and beyond. This is a particularly friendly and cosy house and, considering the size of the kitchen, the choice of dishes seems endless. In the bar area tables may be found in various nooks and crannies. Harking back to earlier times, there's a tiny taproom with a log fire in winter. There is also a small room much appreciated by non-smokers, as well as a large dining room.

In addition to the comprehensive regular menu there are always six or seven specials (all home-cooked) on the weekday menu and nearer to a dozen at weekends. The 'Seafood Basket' is popular – fresh cockles, mussels, prawns and plaice. Modestly-priced jacket potatoes with fillings, salads, freshly-made sandwiches and ploughman's lunches are available and there is a traditional roast meal at mid-day on Sundays. The regular hand-pumped real ales are King and Barnes Sussex and Wadworth 6X, plus three others which change regularly. The draught cider is Taunton and a good selection of wines are available by the glass or bottle. Children are welcome, both in the pub and outside, where there is a large beer garden with amusements. Dogs are permitted, too, as long as they are kept on leads, and this also applies to the garden.

The pub is open on Monday to Saturday from 11 am to 3 pm and 6 pm to 11 pm (summer Saturdays 11 am to 11 pm) and on Sunday from 12 noon to 3 pm and 7 pm to 10.30 pm. Food is served on Monday to Friday from 12 noon to 2.15 pm and 6.45 pm to 9 pm, on Saturday from 12 noon to 2.15 pm and 6.45 pm to 10 pm, and on Sunday from 12 noon to 2.15 pm and 7.30 pm to 9 pm.

Telephone: 01306 631276.

How to get there: Newdigate lies south-east of Dorking and can be reached along country lanes from the A24. Turn eastwards by the Duke's Head in Beare Green and continue for about 1¾ miles to a T-junction where you turn right to the centre of Newdigate. The pub is on the right opposite the church.

Parking: The pub has a car park which you are welcome to use whilst on the walk, but please let someone know. If you are bringing a large group, telephone in advance and it may be possible for the field beyond to be opened up for additional parking.

Length of the walk: 4½ miles. OS maps: Landranger 187 or Pathfinders 1226 and 1227 (inn GR 197420).

Here is a fun steeplechase to test your fitness. Although the entire route is on level ground, at the end of the walk you will have earned a good meal by virtue of the numerous stiles it's necessary to cross. Most of the paths pass over farmland and there are some pretty woods, enhanced by the sound of babbling brooks. Look out, too, for some less usual species of tree.

The Walk

1   From the pub cross the road, passing St Peter's church on your left. Although the church dates from the 13th century its attractive tower and spire of oak shingles were replaced as recently as 1985. Continue along the road and, after passing the last house on the right, turn right over a stile. Bear left across a field to another stile and turn right. Cross the next field to a metal gate and then continue along the

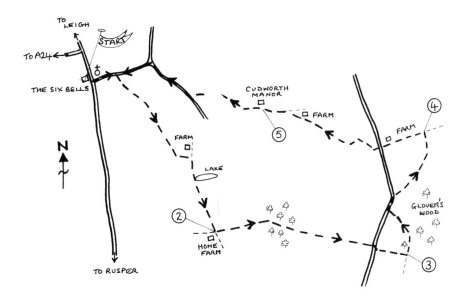

left edge of the next field. Go over a footbridge and straight across the next field to a gate. Bear left across the next field to a stile, with farm buildings over on your left, and reach a farm track. Turn right along the track and shortly pass a lake over on your left. Go through a bridle gate and towards some farm buildings. Pass between the farm buildings and go through a gate out to a driveway. The buildings on the right form Home Farm, which was once a wing of the 16th century Newdigate Place.

2   Immediately turn left by an oak tree, go over a stile, following the direction of the waymark, and head for a stile to the right of a solitary tree. Continue straight ahead, then go over a stile and footbridge into woodland. Bear right across another footbridge then cross the stile ahead. Continue along the right side of a field, turning right over another stile and footbridge. Turn left and climb, following the line of trees, with a stream down on your left. Enter a field and keep to the left edge, later looking for a waymark on a tree to your left. Drop down to cross a stile. Bear right, then go diagonally left across a field to a stile to the left of a garden and pens. You reach a road which you cross diagonally right to a fingerpost. Continue ahead on the tree-lined footpath which ends at a stile leading you onto a crossing track.

3   Turn left onto another path under trees forming part of Glover's Wood. This wood has some unusual species, including wych elm,

69

Cudworth Manor, Newdigate.

small-leaved lime and the wild service tree. As you emerge from the woods into a field bear left and immediately look right for a fenced track running between fields. You come out to a road, turn right and in 100 yards or so turn right again, over a stile by a fingerpost, into a field. Go straight ahead to cross another stile and then go diagonally left across the next field towards yet another. Do not take this first stile but bear left to a double stile leading into another field. Continue along the right perimeter of the field to another stile leading to a farm track.

4 Turn left along the track and, after going through farm buildings, come out to a road. Cross the road to a stile and footpath fingerpost. You now go over several stiles (mostly all helpfully waymarked) and cut the corners of many small fields, too numerous to mention in detail, but generally leading you in a north-westerly direction. Eventually you go past some farm buildings and reach a main bridleway by some houses. Turn left on this track and in about 250 yards you will reach Cudworth Manor.

5 Continue on the track as it bears round to the right and you eventually come out to a road. Turn right along the road and in about ¼ mile reach a junction. Turn left along the road and, in another ¼ mile or so, reach the church and pub in the centre of Newdigate.

15 Brockham
The Dukes Head

The Dukes Head faces onto the great expanse of Brockham Green, the site of Surrey's (reputedly) largest annual Guy Fawkes' bonfire, with Christ Church and its spire over on the other side. Brockham is a name associated with badgers, which used to abound near the river Mole here, but could well mean 'settlement by a brook'. The green was regularly used for cricket and well-known players, including WG Grace, have played here. At one time the village rush-chair maker fashioned straw hats for the home team. The church is comparatively new, dating from 1847.

Some 200 years ago the pub was burnt down. Following the fire it was rebuilt, but parts of the original building remain an attraction to this day, particularly the appealing brick walls. It has been extended and refurbished. The friendly staff and the colourful walls contribute towards a really cosy, relaxed atmosphere. The 'Duke', by the way, was the Duke of Marlborough, the distinguished soldier and ancestor of Winston Churchill.

All the main meals on the specials board are home-made, as well as many of those on the regular menu, which features traditional pub favourites together with the usual jacket potatoes and sandwiches.

The evening menu is larger and includes grills, steaks, chicken dishes and so on. 'Feature Nights' are held – curries on Wednesdays and special steaks on Thursdays and Fridays. A separate children's menu is always available. There is no problem with children or dogs entering the pub and, in addition to the seats outside facing onto the green, there is a beer garden with an aviary at the rear. The real ales on offer are the Ind Coope regulars, Tetley, Friary and Burton, and there is also a guest ale, changed weekly. Olde English draught cider is here along with a good range of wines available by glass or bottle.

The pub is open on Monday to Saturday from 11 am to 2.30 pm and 6 pm to 11 pm, and on Sunday from 12 noon to 3 pm and 7 pm to 10.30 pm. Food is served on Monday to Saturday from 12 noon to 2 pm and 6 pm to 9.30 pm and on Sunday from 12 noon to 2 pm and 7 pm to 9.30 pm.

Telephone: 01737 842023.

How to get there: Brockham is just off the A25, south-east of Dorking. From the M25 leave at junction 8 (travelling clockwise) or junction 9 (anti-clockwise) and make your way to the parallel A25. Brockham is signposted 1 mile from Dorking or 3 miles from Reigate. Once you have crossed the bridge over the river turn left along the green and the pub is just past its near neighbour, the Royal Oak.

Parking: The pub has a large car park which, with permission, you are welcome to use whilst on the walk.

Length of the walk: 3¾ miles. OS maps: Landranger 187 or Pathfinders 1226 and 1227 (inn GR 198496).

Good views of the North Downs and Leith Hill and its surrounds will be constantly in view as you make your way along the paths, mainly through fields. There is no need to climb ... not even the most gentle of slopes.

The Walk

1 From the pub turn right along the green and cross the road to the old village pump with its tiled roof. It was built over a spring as a memorial to Henry Pope who lived nearby at Betchworth House. During the 19th century he was a great benefactor to the village and gave the land for the church. Continue ahead into Old School Lane and over a bridge crossing Tanners Brook which feeds into the nearby river Mole. Almost immediately bear right onto a bridleway, passing a house called Madeira. After about ¼ mile, just before some woodland, look for a stile on the left leading onto a public footpath, part of the Greensand Way.

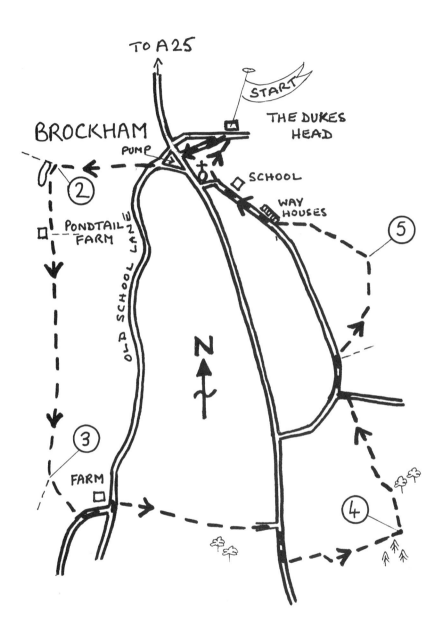

TO A25

START

THE DUKES HEAD

BROCKHAM

PUMP

②

SCHOOL

WAY HOUSES

⑤

PONDTAIL FARM

NEW SCHOOL LANE

OLD SCHOOL

N

③

FARM

④

Village pump, Brockham Green.

2 Go over the stile, passing a pond on your right, and continue along the perimeter of a field. Two stiles take you into the next field and you pass Pondtail Farm on your right. Maintain your southerly direction over four more fields, connected by stiles and plank and concrete bridges, for the best part of another ¾ mile. Having passed some large barns way over on your left, you cross your final stile in the series and enter a fifth field.

3 Now bear left towards a farm track, go over a bridge (potentially muddy), past a house on your right and the barns mentioned earlier on your left. Go through a farm gate onto a narrow concrete road. Turn left, passing more barns on your left, and then bear left to reach another road, which you cross to a very wide bridleway opposite. Eventually the bridleway merges with a residential road and you continue to the end of this to meet a main road. Cross the road and turn right for about 200 yards, where you turn left over a stile onto a public footpath running along the side of a field. Go over a plank bridge into another field and your path curves round to the right to a stile which you **do not** cross. Continue along the field perimeter. Another stile takes you into the next field then, after you have passed a small wood on your right, you will reach a fingerpost.

4 Turn left, passing a footbridge on your right, and make your way along the edge of the same field. You reach the end of some woodland on your right and bear left into the next field with a hedge and ditch on your right. Enter the next field, pass a small copse, and continue into yet another field. The next stile leads you onto a road on which you bear left then turn immediately right onto another road. In about 150 yards you will discover a public footpath on the right, but do not turn here. Continue for just two or three more yards and then bear right onto a public footpath between houses. Go over a stile or through a metal barrier and shortly another path comes in from the right. Continue straight ahead towards a tree with hand-painted 'footpath' signs.

5 Your path turns sharply left and takes you over a bridge, soon passing the back gardens of some houses. Eventually you go between more houses and come out to a road. Cross the road, turn right and immediately look for the four impressive, listed, Victorian houses, named One Way House through to Four Way House. Continue up the road, passing a school, and upon reaching the church bear right past it and across the green back to the pub.

16 Walton on the Hill
The Chequers

The Chequers sits at the southern end of the largely Victorian village of Walton on the Hill, which was mentioned ('Waltone') in the Domesday Book of 1086. The extension 'on the Hill' distinguishes it from Walton-on-Thames. Most of the villages straddling the North Downs lie in the Weald or in valleys but Walton on the Hill sits aloft, some 600 ft above sea level.

Although I could not discover any definite dates, some of the architecture suggests the pub might be fairly old. It is certainly large, with four or five bars and a separate 80-seater restaurant. A smart, comfortable, managed house, it is owned by Young's Brewery of Wandsworth in south-west London. In winter real log fires at each end of the pub warm the temperature and enhance the atmosphere.

Most of the food is home-prepared and cooked and, besides a comprehensive bar menu containing all the usual pub favourites, there is a blackboard with five daily specials, with choices such as deep fried squid rings and macaroni and egg Florentine. The restaurant has a separate menu. Young's Bitter or Special, plus Winter Warmer during the appropriate season, are the real ales. Draught Blackthorn cider and Guinness are there for those who prefer them. The list of wines is extensive and many are available by the glass. There is no problem with either children or dogs entering the pub and, outside, the garden contains play equipment and a boules piste.

The pub is open on Monday to Thursday from 11 am to 3 pm and 5.30 pm to 11 pm, on Friday and Saturday from 11 am to 11 pm, and on Sunday from 12 noon to 3 pm and 7 pm to 10.30 pm. Food is served every day, except Sunday evenings during the winter, from 12 noon to 2.30 pm and 6 pm to 9 pm. Everything on the menus is available at all times, apart from Sunday lunchtimes when a different bar snacks and specials menu is offered. From Easter until October, and whatever the weather, there are barbecued meals in the garden every lunchtime and evening, including Sundays.

Telephone: 01737 812364.

How to get there: If using the M25, leave it at junction 8 and join the A217 going north. Take the B290, signposted to Tadworth and Walton on the Hill, turning left onto the B2220. From Dorking and the A25, approach via the B2032, turning left into Chequers Lane.

Parking: The pub has a large car park which, with permission, you are welcome to use whilst on your walk.

Length of the walk: 3½ miles. OS maps: Landranger 187 or Pathfinder 1207 (inn GR 223550).

Much of the walk is over the wide open spaces of Banstead Heath, an area sandwiched between the M25 and suburbia and much appreciated by local people. This is also horse-riding country and is consequently dominated by bridleways rather than footpaths. If the bridleways are muddy after rain look for drier footpaths running more or less parallel. Many exist but they are too numerous to be described.

The Walk

1   From the pub turn right and take a footpath immediately on the right running alongside the pub. Cross over a lane and continue on the path, with the church over on your left, shortly bearing right on a narrow path between a beech hedge and a fence. Cross over a road and walk on the path running along the side of Nursery Close.

2   You reach a road junction by the entrance of Walton Heath Golf Club and go straight over to the path opposite between white posts. Continue along the side of the golf course, which in 1981 was the venue for the Ryder Cup. The path becomes a tarred driveway and you continue straight ahead to go through concrete posts to the right of a grand white house, Emerald Place. Go over another driveway, into woods and in about 100 yards, at a junction of paths, turn sharp

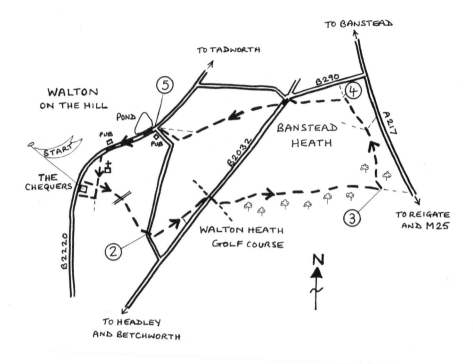

right to a main road, which you cross. Join the public bridleway opposite and, after about 100 yards, reach a fork where you go left on the bridleway, signposted 'Chipstead Lane ⅔ mile'. You reach the open area of Banstead Heath, with woodland on your right. HG Wells once wrote of this area, suggesting it was good sheep and mutton country, but now it is a large public open space, criss-crossed by bridleways but also with a myriad of paths for walkers. You enter a second large open area and at the far side turn right and immediately left, still in the direction of Chipstead Lane, now only ⅓ mile away. Immediately go through a barrier on the right, thus joining a footpath that runs parallel with the bridleway. At the end of the path go through another barrier and rejoin the bridleway for a few yards, where you reach a three-way fingerpost.

3 At this hairpin bend turn sharp left up a slope, on the bridleway signposted 'Mill Road ½ mile', passing a seat over on your right. Ignore several crossing and branching paths and keep to the main track. Later, at a junction of paths continue ahead, passing another seat, and take the right of two parallel paths. Further on you may notice traffic passing along a road ahead. About 100 yards before

St Peter's, Walton on the Hill.

reaching it look for a yellow-waymarked footpath on the left.
4 Turn left on the path, shortly passing an attractive rustic seat and discovering open areas to your right and left. Continue over crossing tracks, probably aware of traffic on a road over to your right. Later your path forks left through a barrier and you shortly come out to an open area and pass another rustic seat on your left. Turn right along the side of the green, passing houses on your left, and reach a road. Cross the road, turn left and in 100 yards or so turn right on a bridleway. Continue ahead over crossing tracks and eventually reach a definite fork. Go left through a barrier onto a path, thus leaving the bridleway. Later pass another rustic seat, go through posts and reach a green where you bear right towards the Blue Boar pub. Continue towards a road and cross to the large pond back in the village of Walton on the Hill.
5 Turn left along the road (Walton Street) passing the village primary school. You pass another pub, the Fox and Hounds, but our chosen pub is only a few more minutes away. Later turn left into Breech Lane, passing The Old Rectory, and arrive at St Peter's church – well worth a visit.

Continue down Breech Lane. In less than 100 yards beyond the path that you took at the start of the walk find a parallel one on the right which will also bring you back to the pub.

⓱ Charlwood
The Greyhound

The Greyhound is one of Charlwood's three pubs, all kept busy due to their proximity to London's second airport at Gatwick. This pleasant village is well endowed with beautiful old houses, some of which are described in the walk instructions.

Following a change of ownership, this Greene King house was completely refurbished at the end of 1994. Although just about everything is new, with smart oak woodwork, nothing is out of character with what one would expect to find in a country pub. The interior is cosy, inviting and relaxed.

The menu, although not massive, is certainly varied and will cover the needs of any hungry walker – or anyone else for that matter! If you require even more choices, check out the specials board and possibly be tempted by one of the jacket potatoes (oven and not microwave cooked) with their range of fillings, or by the traditional roast on Sunday. A special children's menu, called 'King's Lunch Bunch', features favourite food and drinks with innovative names. The real ales come down from East Anglia and, although no guest ale is on offer, the Greene King IPA, Rayments or Abbot Ale should satisfy the most discerning of tastes. Cider drinkers have a choice of either

Blackthorn or Red Rock and stout drinkers can decide between Guinness and Beamish. Wines come by the bottle or glass. Children are welcome as long as they keep away from the bar. There are even high chairs provided for the very young in the non-smoking restaurant area. Well-behaved dogs are also welcome. There is a small garden.

The pub is open on Monday to Saturday from 11 am to 11 pm, and on Sunday from 12 noon to 3 pm and 7 pm to 10.30 pm. Food is served on Monday to Saturday from 12 noon to 2.30 pm and 6 pm to 9.30 pm, and on Sunday from 12 noon to 2.30 pm and 7 pm to 9.30 pm.

Telephone: 01293 862203.

How to get there: Charlwood lies close to the Sussex border and is between Reigate and Crawley. From the Gatwick Airport turn-off leave the M23 at junction 9A for the A23. Exit from the A23 via a roundabout, taking the Charlwood turning. In a little over 2 miles look for the pub on the right as you enter the village from the east.

Parking: The pub has a small car park at the rear and you are welcome to use it whilst on your walk, but please let the landlord know.

Length of the walk: 3½ miles. OS maps: Landranger 187 or Pathfinder 1227 (inn GR 248410).

The route serves as an excellent introduction to Charlwood as many of its most historic buildings are passed on the way. The attractive woodland paths running close to the village are used, too, so one has the best of the rural as well as the urban features of the area. The aircraft leaving nearby Gatwick Airport will make their presence known but should not provide too much of a distraction from the pretty countryside.

The Walk

1 From the pub turn right along the road, passing a turning on the right, Perrylands, until you reach Chapel Road. Turn right along the road and, upon reaching a school, continue ahead on a bridleway for a few yards to Providence chapel on your left. This building was moved from Horsham where it had been used as an army barracks' guardroom at the time when a Napoleonic invasion was threatened. It also looks as if it might have been transported from a Hollywood wild West film set. Retrace your steps to the school and turn right. Continue to the end of this road to have a look at Mores and Swan Cottages and then retrace your steps. Opposite the school turn right on a paved path and shortly pass The Cage on your left. This stone building, now used as a small museum, was once the village lockup.

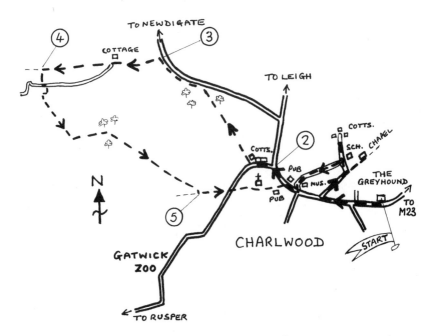

The use of small pieces of black ironstone to decorate uneven mortar joints is a typical Surrey feature, known as galleting. You meet a road and turn right along it, passing the Rising Sun and shortly reaching Rectory Lane on the left, signposted to Rusper and Russ Hill.

2 Turn left along the lane and shortly discover some beautiful cottages on your right. Houseleeks, such as the ones on the low roof on the right of Tudor Cottage, were encouraged by country people who believed they offered protection against witchcraft and fire. Also pass Laurel Cottage, a small 'open hall' cottage built to a medieval plan, then turn right to pass Bristows, or School Cottage as it was previously called. Built around 1620, for over 250 years it was a charity school for boys. Continue along the edge of fields and reach a stile leading you into a snatch of woods and come out to a road, on which you turn left. Soon join a path on the left running parallel with the road and come out to the road near a turning on the left, Beggarshouse Lane.

3 Turn left along the lane and reach Beggars Cottage, where you maintain direction along a bridleway. Continue along the bridleway for about another ¼ mile where you will find a stile on the left.

4 Cross the stile and continue over a field to cross a stile in front of two houses. Turn left along a roadway for a few yards, turning right over another stile. Keep close to the fence on your right and, when it ends, turn left. Continue down the right side of a field, ignoring a

Bristows or School Cottage at Charlwood.

stile by a plank bridge on your right and, at the bottom of the field, cross a stile into a wood. At a fork keep left and later another stile leads you out of the woods. Bear right, keeping alongside the fence on your right. A stile leads you through a snatch of woodland to another stile taking you into a field. As you maintain direction down the field you may hear some unfamiliar bird calls coming from the nearby Gatwick Zoo. The zoo is open from March to October inclusive and many of the exhibits, such as birds and butterflies, are in walk-through areas where you have close contact with them.

Head for the field's bottom left corner where you will find a stile and plank bridge. Continue straight ahead over two more stiles and then go right, out to a lane.

5 Turn left to reach a road and cross to a footpath leading to the golden sandstone church of St Nicholas.

The church has a beautifully carved and painted 15th-century chancel screen, which has been restored to its pristine splendour. In 1962, 13th-century wall paintings, discovered under whitewash in 1858, were painstakingly restored.

Leave the church and continue ahead, passing the Half Moon, until you reach a main road. Turn right along the road, passing Ifield Lane on the right, soon arriving back at the pub.

18 Godstone
The Bell Inn

The Bell Inn is situated in the village of Godstone, still a busy place but much improved since the A22 bypass was constructed some years ago. The large green with its attractive pond has always been a mecca for visitors.

The pub is a charming Grade II listed building, mainly 17th century but with parts going back to the 15th and some even further back to the 14th century. In the bar area, decorated with brass and copper, the beams and fireplace are said to be the originals. Imagine sharing the same area enjoyed by others over 600 years ago! Apart from the bar with its snug there is a conservatory for dining and a separate restaurant. The entire inn was completely refurbished in 1994.

In the restaurant or conservatory there is waitress service and a wide choice from the 'Natterjacks' menu, which includes familiar steaks as well as the more unusual wild boar or even alligator. There's also a children's menu called 'Tadpoles' with puzzles on the back. The atmosphere is relaxed and informal, American-diner style. The bar snacks include sandwiches, jacket potatoes and ploughman's lunches and the blackboard specials may be items such as foccia bread topped with roasted vegetables and mozzarella cheese. Worth trying is the

head chef's award winning 'Seafood Gumbo'. Three real ales come through the pumps, usually Burton, Friary and a third which changes regularly. Draught Guinness is also available. The wine list is comprehensive, the house wines coming by the glass or bottle. Children are, of course, most welcome and there is no problem with dogs as long as they are kept on leads and are well-behaved. At the rear there is a garden which, like the restaurant, gets very busy on summer weekends.

The pub is open on Monday to Saturday from 11 am to 11 pm and on Sunday from 12 noon to 10.30 pm. Food is served all the time but pre-booking is advisable from Friday to Sunday.

Telephone: 01883 743133.

How to get there: If using the M25, leave it at junction 6 and follow the road to Godstone. The pub is on the right-hand side just beyond the green. Godstone, which is between Redhill and Oxted, is also reached via the A25.

Parking: There are two or three car parks on the green which you can use if the pub's one is full. Providing you are using the pub before or after your walk, you are welcome to use its car park, but please seek permission first.

Length of the walk: 2½ miles. OS maps: Landranger 187 or Pathfinder 1207 (inn GR 351515).

There's something for everyone on this short ramble – an appealing village green, a large lake with diverse bird-life, a charming church, more lakes and a farm to visit with unusual attractions for children. The route is suitable for any time of the year.

The Walk

1 From the pub cross the road and turn left. As you walk along the pavement look for a florist's which was at one time a butcher's shop, complete with traditional window shutters. You soon arrive at another old inn, the White Hart, and turn right on the public footpath, shortly reaching the Bay Pond Nature Reserve. You reach a road but, before going through the lychgate into the churchyard, walk a few yards to your right to see the ornate St Mary's almshouses.

As you pass the church, which is dedicated to St Nicholas, you may not appreciate that it is only 100 or so years old, although the foundations date from the 12th century. In the churchyard, if you have time, seek out the gravestone of the appropriately named Walker Miles. You'll find it on a grassy slope, looking oddly out of place amongst its neighbours. No formal tombstone this, but a natural,

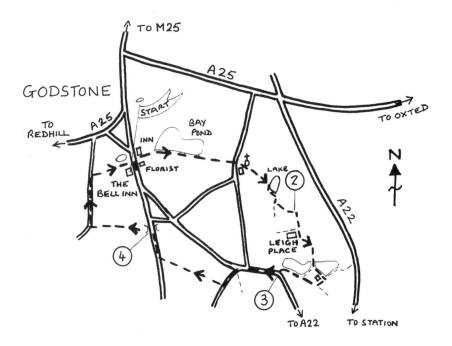

unhewn sarsen obelisk that could have strayed from a Dartmoor stone circle. Walker Miles' real name was Edmund Taylor and he walked many thousands of miles of paths in England, particularly in Surrey, Kent and Sussex. Around 100 years ago he produced some 40 walking guides, forerunners, perhaps, of books like this one! He was a founder member of the London Rambling Club from which, along with others, the Ramblers' Association was later formed.

Leave the churchyard and continue ahead on a footpath, shortly passing a pleasing lake on your left. The path soon turns right and then bears left up a slope, alongside an avenue of conifers, leading to Leigh Place, a Jacobean house built by John Evelyn. Turn left past a brick wall and enter a field through an archway of trees.

2 Turn right along the side of the field and come down to a fingerpost. Bear left onto a bridleway, shortly reaching a three-way fingerpost and a stile on the right. Cross over the stile, proceed between two lakes and soon reach another three-way fingerpost. Turn left over another stile and pass Leigh Mill House on your right. You reach some garages and turn right, following the direction of a fingerpost. At a T-junction turn right and soon go across a ford. If the stream is in full flood you can use the footbridge. Come out to a road.

3 Turn right along the pavement and, just before you go over a

St Mary's Almshouses, Godstone.

turning on the right, look across the road for an old milestone. Soon cross the road and turn left up a road past some white-painted cottages, ignoring the immediate footpath on the left. In 100 yards or so turn right at a fingerpost onto a public footpath which is narrow and possibly overgrown. Continue along an embankment, with a stream down on your right, climb some steps, go over a stile and then over another stile. This takes you into a part of Godstone Farm, a working farm and recreational area for children, which is open during the summer months. Bear right past a log 'bridge' and pass a barn on your left, continuing on a farm track. Later pass the farm car park on your left, go over another stile and down to a road, where there's another stile to cross, or you may use a gate. Turn right along Tilburstow Hill Road, an old Roman road, and just before you reach a bridge cross over to a public footpath.

4 Turn left on the footpath, with a stream on your right, and continue along the right perimeter of a field. Towards the top of the field bear right over a ditch and go along the side of the next field. You progress along a tarred path by the side of a house and come out to a lane. Turn right and in about ¼ mile arrive back at Godstone green, where you turn right again, back to the pub.

⓳ Chelsham
The Bull Inn

The Bull Inn, although close to Croydon and south-east Greater London, has found itself a delightful rural setting on Chelsham Common, adjoining a little-explored piece of countryside.

The pub has been refurbished and is clean and comfortable without being pretentious. There are plenty of tables in the bar and there is also a pleasant, separate dining area. The menu has all the usual pub grub, such as salads, several choices of plain and toasted sandwiches, ploughman's lunches, jacket potatoes and so on. For lunchtime diners there is a blackboard showing three daily specials of home-cooked food, for example, curries and pasta dishes. For Sunday lunch you can choose from two roasts and two other traditional meals. Children's portions are available. The regular real ales include Worthington and Bass and there are two or three guest ales. Besides draught Dry Blackthorn cider and draught Guinness, Thomas Caffrey's Irish Ale, actually brewed in the Emerald Isle, is on tap. An unusual feature is the information blackboards describing the ales in detail. Worthington, for example, is described as 'A fairly malty light coloured beer with a somewhat bitter finish. A pleasant drinking beer.' If you prefer wine, there are three house wines available by the glass and others sold by the bottle. There are no problems with children or dogs entering the pub, as long as they are on their best behaviour. There is a garden to use with a slide and other equipment for children.

The pub is open on Monday to Saturday from 11 am to 3 pm and 5.30 pm to 11 pm, and on Sunday from 12 noon to 3 pm and 7 pm to 10.30 pm. Food is served on Monday to Saturday from 12 noon to 2.30 pm and 6 pm to 10 pm, and on Sunday from 12 noon to 2.30 pm and 7 pm to 9 pm. On Tuesday to Saturday evenings there is also a 'Chef's Menu' with steaks. The bar menu is available on Sunday and Monday evenings.

Telephone: 01883 622970.

How to get there: Turn off the B269 (Warlingham – Limpsfield road) at the Sainsbury store, into Chelsham Road. In less than a mile you will discover the pub facing you across the green.

Parking: The pub has adequate parking, which you are welcome to use whilst on your walk, but please let the staff know.

Length of the walk: 2½ miles. OS maps: Landranger 187 or Pathfinders 1207 and 1191 (inn GR 372590).

This may not be one of Surrey's more obvious areas for walking but there are some little-used, yet nonetheless pleasant, woodland paths and a country lane leading to one of the county's oldest churches. Although the route is completely flat, you are quite high up and there are sweeping views to enjoy on a fine day.

The Walk

1 From the pub turn left across the car park and then immediately left again to join a grassy path, shortly passing a pond on your right. You reach a road and turn right, soon reaching a crossroads, where you go left. In a little less than 100 yards turn left on a public footpath, soon passing some garages on your left. As you reach a barrier of large logs, turn right to join a narrow path, with an old wire fence on your left. Your path may be overgrown and barely discernible in parts, but if you keep close to the fence there should be no problems. When, after about ¼ mile, the fence reaches a corner, continue straight ahead going through some narrow posts to the right of a gate and onto a bridleway.

2 Turn left on the bridleway and continue, with woods on your left and a mixture of woodland and fields on the right. If you look carefully into the woods you will spot an assault course used for management trainees and, if walking on a weekday, maybe even see them completing their initiative tasks. After about ½ mile on the

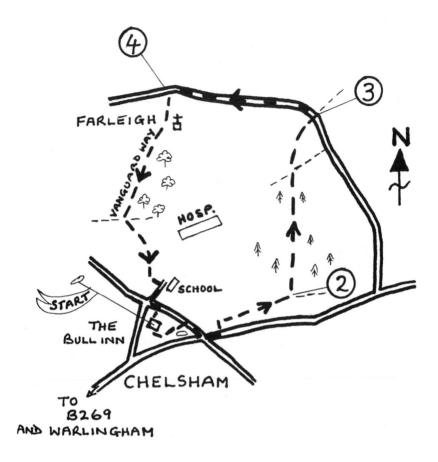

bridleway, as it curves right, you will find a path coming in from the left. A few yards beyond this take a left turn leading to a stile. After crossing the stile head straight across a field towards an opening in the trees and then bear right towards a stile on the other side of the next field. Cross over a common, pass through a small car park and reach a narrow lane, with more common land beyond.

3 Turn left along the lane, which affords good views ahead and across to the Croydon area on the right. You will reach the settlement of Farleigh Court, comprising a few houses, farm buildings and a riding stable. (The hamlet of Farleigh is another ¼ mile further down the lane.)

4 At the sign for St Mary's church turn left on the public footpath. You soon reach this gem of a Norman church, with its shingled bell

St Mary's church, Farleigh.

turret. Almost the entire building dates back over 800 years. Go through the gate into the churchyard, where, if you are ready for a rest, you will find some seats on the left. (If you would like to see the inside of the church, you may collect a key from a local resident whose name and address is on the inner door.) Leave the churchyard and bear left on the bridleway running between fences. This path forms part of the Vanguard Way – a long distance trail running from East Croydon to Seaford Head on the Sussex coast. At the end of the wood on your left leave the bridleway by turning left through a metal barrier onto a footpath, soon going under a water pipe. Go under a bridge and come out to a road, with Warlingham Park School ahead and Warlingham Park Hospital on your left. Cross the road, turn right and then immediately left, back to the road leading to the pub.

20 Dormansland
The Plough

The Plough is a popular pub with walkers as it is open virtually all day long – and that includes Sundays! Dormansland is located in the south-east corner of the county and is close to the borders of East and West Sussex and Kent. It's such a small place that many people regularly walking, or even residing, in Surrey may not have visited or even heard of it before. The village comprises little more than an assortment of cottages and houses strung along a main road, but there are two noteworthy buildings nearby, one of which we pass on the walk. The other is Old Surrey Hall, about 2 miles south-east of the village, which was considerably renovated in the 1920s but goes back to 1450.

The pub, comfortable and with character, has parts dating from the 15th century. The resident ghost is known as Black Alice and the landlady may be able to point out one of the locals who can tell you more about her! Besides the bar, there's a back lounge, with comfy chesterfields and a pleasant restaurant. This Whitbread house has a good selection of food, including grills, fish, jacket potatoes, vegetarian dishes and lighter meals, such as ploughman's lunches and sandwiches. The children have their own menu. There is also a frequently changing 'Chef's Specials Board', which always includes a variety of dishes. You might find beef, celery and walnut pie or poached salmon steak with prawn and pineapple sauce. Beef and mushroom steamed pudding is very popular as are the chef's curries for which he blends his own spices. There are some delicious sweets, and no less than seven different ice-creams. The regular real ales are Flowers, London Pride and Fremlins and there is a weekly changing guest beer. Tea, as well as coffee, is offered, particularly useful between 3 pm and 7 pm on Sundays, when the sale of alcoholic drinks is barred unless you are dining. Apart from around the bar area, children are welcome inside the pub but dogs are not.

The pub is open on Monday to Saturday from 11 am to 11 pm, and on Sunday from 12 noon to 10.30 pm. Food is served on Monday to Saturday from 11 am to 2.30 pm and 7 pm to 9.30 pm (7 pm to 10 pm on Friday and Saturday), and on Sunday from 12 noon to 9 pm (8 pm in winter).

Telephone: 01342 832933.

How to get there: The village is situated a mile or two north of East Grinstead, which is in West Sussex. If coming from the north, leave the M25 at junction 6 and follow the A22 south. Turn left on the B2029 through Lingfield and join the B2028, then take the left fork after a railway bridge, still on the B2028. You will find the pub on the right, 500 yards further on.

Parking: The pub has an adequate car park, which you are welcome to use whilst on your walk, but please seek permission.

Length of the walk: The full route, the longest in the book, is about 5½ miles. However, this may easily be reduced to around 4 miles. OS maps: Landranger 187 or Pathfinder 1228 (inn GR 406428).

This is a ramble on which you will be walking at a height allowing excellent views over the Weald and towards the North Downs, though hardly conscious of the ascent. The full route takes you up Dry Hill, the site of an ancient, pre-Roman, fort. Both routes take in an impressive mansion which, if you time it right, you can visit, too.

The Walk

1 Turn right from the pub and immediately right again down Ford Manor Road, passing some fine cottages on your way. In about 300 yards you reach a fork. Keep left, ignoring an immediate left turn, and shortly reach the farm buildings at Woodgate. Bear right, past a cart shed on your right, going through a farm gate and along the right side of a field to another gate. Enter the next field and turn left along the

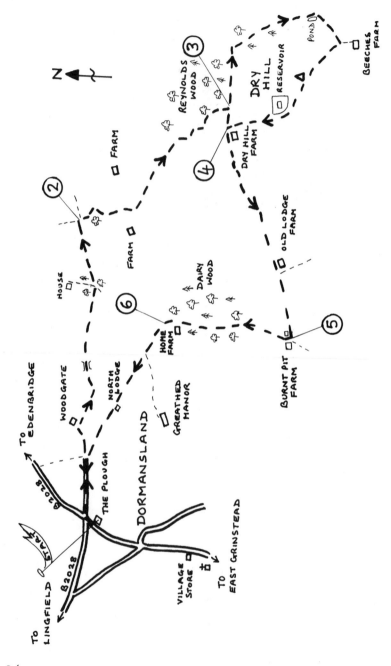

Cottages in Dormansland.

perimeter and past a footbridge. Continue along the perimeter path and cross a stile and a bridge taking you over a stream. Continue ahead and, as the field ends, enter some woodland. Go straight ahead over a track leading to a house over on your left, and then climb a stile, possibly marked with a yellow band. Continue along the edge of the next field, with a hedge and ditch on your right, and arrive at a T-junction and a post with waymarks.

2 Turn right and immediately ignore a path turning off on your left. Your path ascends slightly. It's a bridleway so it may be muddy. It curves left, then right around some woods and comes to a T-junction. There are farmhouses over to your left and right. You turn right and, almost immediately, go through a farm gate on the left. Use the left one of two more farm gates and go across a field. Enter some woodland via an old gateway and continue through Reynolds Wood. Later you'll find fields, in fact former orchards, on your right as the path twists and turns along the edge of the wood. At the top of a slope you arrive at some farm buildings. Stop here and look back at the marvellous views across the Weald towards the Downs. After passing a house on your right, you reach a crossing track. This is a section of the Sussex Border Path.

If you wish to take the shorter route, turn right here past some houses at Dry Hill Farm, shortly reaching a track coming in from the left. Continue with the instructions at point 4.

3 *For the longer route,* turn left along the track and, at the end of a plum tree orchard, go through a gateway into a wood and immediately turn right into the trees onto a potentially muddy path. You shortly reach a junction of paths where you turn right by a three-way marker post. If it was previously muddy, the path may become a little firmer now, for at least some of the way. You reach a fork and keep right (bridleway '650') and come up to a pretty pond which you pass on your right. As you pass a bridle gate on your left you should be enjoying some extremely fine views as the path continues along the edge of the wood, with fields to the left. You are right on the Kent border now and, for a few yards, actually cross over it. The path becomes surfaced as it winds round a garden and you reach a T-junction, turning right, away from a farmhouse (Beeches Farm). Enter a field and go through a gateway into another and on to the summit of Dry Hill. As you pass along the left side of the field you will probably notice a triangulation pillar on the right. The metal railings ahead mark the boundary of a reservoir and the bracken area opposite is the site of an Iron Age fort. Continue down a field, formerly an orchard, and arrive at the buildings of Dry Hill Farm. Turn left on a roadway.

4 Pass more farm buildings and in about ½ mile reach Old Lodge Farm. The Sussex Border Path turns off left here, but you continue ahead on the farm road for another ¼ mile to arrive at Burnt Pit Farm.

5 Immediately after the first barn, turn right through a gate. Go over a stile by a gate and bear right, then over another stile (or through a convenient gate) and enter Dairy Wood. Continue over a brick bridge and you are eventually led down to the dilapidated buildings of Home Farm.

6 After passing the house, bear left and shortly reach a junction of tarred tracks and bear right.

Over on your left is Greathed Manor, which was previously called Ford Manor. It was built by Robert Kerr, who wrote *The Gentleman's House*, in 1868. It is still a private residence but has been turned into several apartments for gentlefolk. It is open to visitors from May to September, on Wednesdays and Thursdays between 2 pm and 5 pm.

You reach North Lodge and continue ahead on the tar to arrive at a junction, where you bear left along the road and retrace your steps back to the pub.